Your Sorrow
Is My Sorrow

Your Sorrow
Is My Sorrow

Hope and Strength in Times of Suffering

Joyce Rupp

Illustrations by Mary Southard

A Crossroad Book
The Crossroad Publishing Company
New York

The Crossroad Publishing Company
370 Lexington Avenue, New York, NY 10017

Copyright © 1999 by Joyce Rupp

Text art by Mary Southard, CSJ, copyright © 1999 Sisters of St. Joseph of La Grange

Cover art by Ted (Ettore) De Grazia, copyright © 1963 by De Grazia Foundation, Tucson, Ariz.

Printed in the United States of America

Library of Congress Cataloging-in-Publication Data

Rupp, Joyce.
    Your sorrow is my sorrow : hope and strength in times of suffering / by Joyce Rupp ; illustrations by Mary Southard.
       p.   cm.
    Includes bibliographical references.
    ISBN 0-8245-1566-8
    1. Sorrows of the Blessed Virgin Mary, Devotion to.
2. Suffering – Religious aspects – Catholic Church. 3. Consolation.
I. Title.
BX2161.5.S6 R87 1999
242'.4 – dc21   98-31344

1   2   3   4   5   6   7   8   9   10   04   03   02   01   00   99

For the members of my religious community
the Servants of Mary
in gratitude for our shared history
and our devotion to the Sorrows of Mary

and

For my mother
Hilda Wilberding Rupp
who has held many sorrows in her arms
while always remaining
a woman of hope and joy

CONTENTS

THE SEVEN SORROWS OF MARY

The First Sorrow: The Prophecy of Simeon

Guided by the Spirit, Simeon came into the temple; and when the parents brought in the child Jesus, to do for him what was customary under the law, Simeon took him in his arms and praised God. . . . Then Simeon blessed them and said to his mother, Mary: "This child is destined for the falling and the rising of many in Israel, and to be a sign that will be opposed so that the inner thoughts of many will be revealed — and a sword will pierce your own soul too." (Luke 2:27–35)

The Second Sorrow: The Flight into Egypt

. . . an angel of the Lord appeared to Joseph in a dream and said, "Get up, take the child and his mother, and flee to Egypt, and remain there until I tell you; for Herod is about to search for the child, to destroy him." Then Joseph got up, took the child and his mother by night, and went to Egypt, and remained there until the death of Herod. (Matt. 2:13–15)

The Third Sorrow: The Loss of the Child Jesus in the Temple

When the festival was ended and they started to return, the boy Jesus stayed behind in Jerusalem, but his parents did not know it. Assuming that he was in the group of travelers, they went a day's journey. Then they started to look for him among their relatives and friends. When they did not find him, they returned to Jerusalem to search for him. After three days they found him in the temple, sitting among the teachers.... When his parents saw him they were astonished; and his mother said to him, "Child, why have you treated us like this? Look, your father and I have been searching for you in great anxiety." He said to them, "Why were you searching for me? Did you not know that I must be in my Father's house? But they did not understand what he said to them. Then he went down with them and came to Nazareth, and was obedient to them. His mother treasured all these things in her heart." (Luke 2:43–51)

The Fourth Sorrow: Mary Meets Jesus Carrying His Cross

A great number of the people followed him, and among them were women who were beating their breasts and wailing for him. (Luke 23:27)

The Fifth Sorrow: Mary Stands beneath the Cross of Jesus

Meanwhile, standing near the cross of Jesus were his mother, and his mother's sister, Mary the wife of Clopas, and Mary Magdalene. When Jesus saw his mother and the disciple whom he loved standing beside her, he said to his mother, "Woman, here is your son." Then he said to the disciple, "Here is your mother." (John 19:25–27)

The Sixth Sorrow: Mary Receives the Dead Body of Jesus

Joseph of Arimathea, who was a disciple of Jesus, though a secret one because of his fear of the Jews, asked Pilate to let him take away the body of Jesus. Pilate gave him permission; so he came and removed his body. (John 19:38)

The Seventh Sorrow: Jesus Is Laid in the Tomb

Nicodemus, who had at first come to Jesus by night, also came, bringing a mixture of myrrh and aloes, weighing about a hundred pounds. They took the body of Jesus and wrapped it with the spices in linen cloths, according to the burial custom of the Jews. Now there was a garden in the place where he was crucified, and in the garden there was a new tomb in which no one had ever been laid. And so, because it was the Jewish day of Preparation, and the tomb was nearby, they laid Jesus there. (John 19:39–42)

PREFACE

It is the feast of Mary, Mother of Sorrows. I am on the coast of Maine, relishing two weeks of solitude for writing and reflection. Today I begin this book on the Seven Sorrows of Mary. I think it is more than a co-incidence that two days ago, on the very day I arrived at this place of strong beauty, the owner of the cottage here was experiencing one of the sorrows of Mary.

Like Mary holding her dead son in her compassionate arms, Jo Betsy held her dying husband, Victor, in hers. She had lovingly and patiently accompanied him on the long journey of tests and treatments for brain cancer, finding hope and losing hope, over and over. On the day I came to her summer home in Maine, she kissed her beloved Victor one last goodbye in Austin, Texas.

Experiences of sorrow such as this have led me to write about the seven traditional sorrows of Mary of Nazareth. Whether or not anyone has any affiliation or devotion to the mother of Jesus, I have come to believe that everyone can find their struggles and sadness hidden in the folds of Mary's robe of sorrows. Whether Mary is approached as a historical or symbolic figure of compassion, the heartaches and sorrows of her life contain a message of strength and encouragement for those who hurt.

I have personally found much hope and inspiration when I have dis-covered my own struggles reflected in the sorrows of Mary. I have felt comfort and kinship in knowing that Mary has been there before me. In this Mother of Sorrows I have found a woman of compassion and courage whose life experiences give me strength to weather my own tribulations.

It is with this conviction that I approach the seven sorrows of Mary. May you be given what you need for your own life's journey as you find your sorrows reflected in those of Mary.

Penobscot Bay
Camden, Maine
September 15, 1997

ACKNOWLEDGMENTS

The content of this book has been greatly shaped by the women in my community who contributed their wisdom in our monthly discussions and by their own written thoughts and feelings about the sorrows of Mary. I consider them co-authors of *Your Sorrow Is My Sorrow*. A few were unable to join us for these gatherings but still offered me suggestions and resources that assisted in my reflection on the seven sorrows of Mary. It is with deep gratitude that I thank each of these sisters of my Servite community:

Veronica Marie Balazs	Mary Anthony Matz
Cecile Marie Bissonnette	Callista McNamara
Clementia Dressel	Cleopha Murphy
Eleanor Galt	Kathleen O'Sullivan
Rosalie Helinsky	Anne Marie Petrylka
Camilla Huber	Mercedes Rapp
Virginia Holland	Catherine Rupp
Audrey Jauron	Christina Rupp
Celeste Lawler	Helen M. Spengler
Barbara Loomis	Barbara Tripp
Bernadette Lubischer	Violet Mae Walker

Adolorata Watson

I also extend special thanks to the following:

– Felicity McKeon, OSM, and Terese Lux, OSM, whose Servite leadership has given me both support and inspiration for my work.

– Janet Barnes, Carola Broderick, Sandra Bury, William John Fitzgerald, Patricia Sloan Skinner, and Ginny Silvestri, OSM, who generously gave of their time and expertise to read my first draft and offer suggestions.

– Marjorie and Jack Ferren, who offered me time at their summer residence on Cape Cod; Corinne LaRoche, who cheered me on while I was there; Jo Betsy Szebehely, who shared her home on Penobscot Bay in Maine; Paula D'Arcy and Macrina Weiderkehr, whose presence brought me such joy during my writing time there.

– Erin King and Maryknoll sister Jean Fallon, without whose help I would never have traveled to the shrine in Kamakura to find the beautiful Kanon.

– All who found the time and courage to share their life stories with me, each a treasure that needed a voice.

– Michael Leach, whose publishing enthusiasm and honesty were such vital components for me as I worked on this book, and John Eagleson, who amazes me with his finely honed editing skills and his ability to create a work of art from a simple manuscript.

– Mary Southard, CSJ, who graciously created her artistic pieces of beauty so all of us can reflect more deeply and fully on the sorrows of Mary.

– Linda Rudkin, who never failed to help me with computer and secretarial needs, always adding a cheerful note to my writing days.

– All who remain unnamed but who were a source of hope, encouragement, inspiration, and support as I wrote this book: How blessed I am to have you in my life!

INTRODUCTION

I never expected to be swept back into my own spiritual tradition when I visited a Buddhist temple in Japan. I was in Tokyo for a conference and decided to visit the city of Kamakura, well known for its abundance of temples and shrines. I knew nothing about this holy place, but when I opened my tour guide book and read about it, something compelled me to go there. I felt particularly drawn to the temple of Kanon, a female deity of boundless compassion and mercy. As I stepped into the train bound for Kamakura I had no idea how deeply the visit would affect my inner world.

The temple sits on a hill with a sweeping view of the sea. It was late January and gentle plum blossoms filled the greening trees within the temple area. Small delicate ponds and carefully tended gardens welcomed me as I entered. The beauty encouraged silence. I moved quietly toward the building that houses the large statue of Kanon (also known as Kannon or Kwannon). I walked into the main sanctuary and saw Kanon for the first time. There before me was a twenty-nine-foot statue carved from a single piece of camphorwood. The beautiful face of the statue easily evokes the quality of lovingkindness that Buddhists attribute to Kanon, whom they refer to as "Boundless Compassion."* The unusual feature of Kanon is not

---

*The practice of lovingkindness is a central part of the Buddhist way. The compassion of Christianity and the lovingkindness of Buddhism are sisters on the spiritual path. Sharon Salzberg describes lovingkindness as "the embrace that allows no separation between self, others, and events — the affirmation and honoring of a core goodness in others and oneself" (Sharon Salzberg, *LovingKindness: The Revolutionary Art of Happiness* [Boston: Shambhala, 1995], ix).

19

her size, however, but rather the eleven small heads that surround the crown of her own large head. Each face has a different expression of the many emotions of those who suffer: sadness, hurt, fear, shock, frustration, grief, worry. . . . It is easy to sense her immense kinship with the suffering ones of the world.

I stood before Kanon for a long, long time. I thought of the many religions, since ancient times, that have a female deity who encompasses the quality of compassion. Then I felt my heart find its place in my own spiritual tradition as I sensed an immense and awesome kinship with Mary of Nazareth. My Christian knowledge and experience of Mary as the "Mother of Sorrows" flooded my awareness. Tears came to my eyes as I recalled how often I had found comfort and hope in Mary as a woman of compassion. It was so clear to me when I stood before Kanon how Mary of Nazareth had become an exemplar of faith, a strong and vivid mentor of lovingkindness for me. I realized, as never before, how deeply I regard her as a feminine ancestor with much to teach me about the way she entered into the transformational events of her life.

When I entered my religious community as a young woman, I was unaware that the central devotion of "the seven sorrows" framed the heart of our spiritual life. I didn't know that in our earliest years in France we were known as "sisters of compassion." As a Servant of Mary, or Servite as we are more commonly called, I have since often joined with my community members in reflecting upon the seven sorrows of Mary. In doing so, we have always kept in perspective the joys of Mary, for she was certainly a woman of joy as well as a woman of sorrow. Her life held deep and sustaining happiness: the gift of her own life and the wonders of each new day, a loving relationship with her husband, Joseph, the birth of a beautiful child, the pleasure of helping this child learn and grow, giving him the security of a loving home, plus the friendships and enjoyable times with other adults that a caring and loving woman like Mary would have had.

In focusing on the sorrows of Mary, it is important to keep in mind that it is Mary's *whole* life of transitions (joys and sorrows) that opened her heart, that drew her into being a woman of kindness, that kept calling her to go deeper in love and to trust the divine presence who was always with her.

Mary as the Embodiment of Compassion

Although Christians do not equate Mary with divinity, they recognize the special relationship she has with the divine. Mary is the feminine embodiment of the divine quality of compassion. For centuries she has been given the title "Mother of Sorrows" or "Our Lady of Sorrows" because of the heartaches she experienced as the mother of Jesus and because her sorrows symbolize the many pains that continue to pierce human lives today. Mary standing at the foot of the cross of her son clearly portrays the compassionate person who enters fully into the pain of another.

Compassion is about being with others in their suffering. It is about entering into that pain in such a way that one is no longer an observer but an integral participant. Compassion does not mean "feeling sorry" for someone. Rather, compassion is to "get inside the skin" of the one who hurts, to experience with him or her the pain that is there, to sense a kinship with the one who is suffering. Before we can be compassionate with others we must first enter our own suffering and extend lovingkindness to ourselves.

True compassion insists that we enter into the sufferings of others. Yet, we cannot become so absorbed by someone else's pain that we cease to have a life of our own. There is a delicate balance between these two dimensions, and sometimes life is such that this delicate balance is shattered. The intensity of someone's painful situation can be so demanding that it swallows our emotional life for a time.

I believe this happened to Mary of Nazareth in her seven great sorrows. Each one threw her off balance. Each one initially grabbed her peace by the throat and shook her spirit violently. Each one demanded her full attention. She gave herself totally to the hurts associated with her son, but she also knew how to dip deeply inside and draw from the strength that the Holy One gave her. Mary's life contained piercing hurts, but it also held a vast reservoir of faith.

Suffering sears us and compassion transforms us. After the storm has passed and the pain has ceased, wisdom and tenderness often bloom in the garden of our hearts. These flowers of compassion begin to bud when we are at the foot of the cross. The juice of our steadfast faithfulness and generous presence fills the buds and eventually opens them in fullness. Mary's compassion held this fruitfulness. Her presence with the disciples in the upper room before Pentecost speaks of her ability to be there for others who were caught up in their suffering and loss.

The Seven Sorrows of Mary

There are several ways to view Mary. Each or all of these can be helpful, depending on our needs and our own mode of spirituality. First, we have "the historical Mary." This is the woman who gave birth to the Jewish teacher and healer who came to be known as Jesus of Nazareth. Secondly, we have "the scriptural Mary." Here we see Mary in relation to Jesus and her inner life of reflection and faith. Thirdly, we have "the legendary Mary." This is the Mary whose life events are told not from Scripture but from stories passed down from age to age.

The seven traditional sorrows of Mary are gleaned from the sparse scriptural references and from legends. The Scriptures tell us little about Mary of Nazareth. We have only a few passages here and there to lead us to her. Much of what Mary is known for comes from these brief mentions. While most of the sorrows attributed to Mary are taken from these snatches of Scripture, several of the sorrows are assumed because of the unfolding events at the time of the death of her son. Of the traditional seven sorrows of Mary three are from legend: Mary meeting Jesus on the road to Calvary, Mary receiving the body of her son when he is taken down from the cross, and Mary being present when Jesus is placed in the tomb.

Besides viewing Mary through history, Scripture, and legend, we can approach her in yet another way. We can see Mary as symbolic of ourselves and others. Thomas Merton writes that Mary is the mother of the Christ in us. Beatrice Bruteau suggests that Mary is the mothering principle in us, a part of us that compassionates and cares for us. C. G. Jung wrote of Mary as a symbol of the eternal feminine, open, receptive, nurturing, and loving.*

The qualities of Mary as the eternal feminine are symbolic of the qualities within us, whether we are male or female. Likewise, her sorrows can also be metaphors for the difficulties we experience in our lives. By entering into Mary's sorrows we can find there a vast resource of courage and wisdom. These painful pieces of Mary's life can enable us to find mean-

---

*See Beatrice Bruteau, *The Easter Mysteries* (New York: Crossroad, 1995), 96–98.

ing and inspiration. They can help us get through our own rough-edged moments.

The Seven Sorrows: Containers of Our Own Life Struggles

The sorrowful events and experiences attributed to Mary's life often relate directly to our own. For example, parents whose children are lost, into crime, murdered, or suffering from a serious illness know how much their sorrow is in kinship with Mary's. At other times her sorrows are indirectly or symbolically connected to ours. We do not have to be a parent to walk in the footsteps of the sorrowful mother. The sufferings of every individual, man or woman, are reflected in some aspect of Mary's sorrows.

Anyone who has ever received news that brought with it a prediction of future turmoil and pain has been there with Mary when Simeon foretold the heartache she would have. Anyone who has ever made a decision to leave a situation that was harmful and destructive has been there with Mary when she fled into Egypt to save her son's life. Anyone who has ever searched with panic and dismay over the loss of a valued part of their life has been there with Mary when she hunted for her missing child. Anyone who has ever met suffering on a deeper level has been there with Mary when she met her suffering son on his path to Calvary. Anyone who has ever vigiled at the bedside of a dying one has been there with Mary as she stood beneath the cross. Anyone who has ever embraced a part of their life that has died has been there with Mary when she received the dead body of her child in her arms. Anyone who has ever stood in a cemetery with tears clutching at their heart has been there with Mary when she watched her son being laid to rest in the tomb.

As we enter into these sorrows we see how Mary questioned and grappled with what was confusing and unclear, how she needed others to be there with her in her pain, how she reflected on her life experiences in order to find meaning in them. We also see her inner resiliency, how her faith sustained her, and how her deep love for her son gave her strength to enter into and endure her suffering. We see how she never gave up even in her most desolate of times. As we walk with Mary in her sorrows we discover that we are not alone in what is most difficult for us. In Mary we have a mother, a sister, a mentor, a friend.

Gathering the Wisdom of the Elders

As part of the preparation for writing this book, I traveled two and a half hours to my Servite motherhouse one day each month for seven months to meet with the elders of my community. I invited them to reflect with me on one of the seven sorrows of Mary. At each meeting we tried to "get inside the skin" of Mary. We tried to "be Mary." We described to each other what we thought she could have been thinking and feeling at that time. We wondered aloud about what her dreams and longings might have been. Most of all, we slipped inside the pain of Mary. It was there that we related Mary's sorrow to our own sorrow. Then we asked how this sorrow was evident in the people we knew and in the larger world. Many events and situations leapt into our conversation. It was astounding how easily we found connections and similarities.

After each time of gathering, we took three weeks apart to ponder, to reflect more fully, and to write prayers. Some wrote profusely; others wrote nothing at all. It did not matter. I gratefully received the gift of their presence as well as each morsel of their verbal and written contributions. The shared wisdom of these elders is the juice that feeds the content of the chapters that I have written and the prayers that follow.*

---

*I also asked participants at retreats and conferences that I led to send me their life stories of how one of the sorrows of Mary related to their lives. I am deeply indebted to each one who found the courage and took the time to share their sorrows with me. All names in the stories have been changed in order to protect the anonymity of individuals, but the quotes I use are directly from either conversations or letters from these women and men.

Your Sorrow
Is My Sorrow

The First Sorrow:
The Prophecy of Simeon

THE FORETELLING OF SORROW

"This child is destined for the falling and the rising of many in Israel, and to be a sign that will be opposed so that the inner thoughts of many will be revealed — and a sword will pierce your own soul too." (Luke 2:34)

Mary Speaks

I thought the worst was behind me — the struggles with Joseph before our marriage, the strenuous, hurried journey to help my cousin Elizabeth when I wasn't feeling very well myself, and that terrifying day when my contractions began while Joseph and I were traveling. How I had hoped that life would grow calm and serene when I beheld that beautiful child of ours at his birth. It did seem to be that way for a while.

I felt contented with life the day that Joseph and I walked into the temple with our young son. I never expected it to be anything but happy as we went to present Jesus according to customary Jewish law. As we completed the ritual, one of the elders named Simeon came to us with a look of recognition on his face. Neither of us had met him before, so I hesitated a moment when he asked to hold our small son. But there was an aura of wisdom and depth about his presence, so I placed Jesus in his frail arms.

I saw a tear fall out of the crinkled corner of the old man's eye as he held our son. He lifted Jesus as high as his aging arms could stretch and proclaimed that Jesus would be a radiant guide for others. He said Jesus was going to make a great difference for many people. I looked at Joseph at the same time as he looked at me. We were both smiling at what Simeon had just said.

I didn't understand Simeon's tear until he spoke again. This time he looked directly at me. Again I saw the depth beyond his eyes. His voice trembled and his words were engulfed with sadness as he said to me, "This child will face great opposition. He will not be accepted by those who have power to destroy him. This child will pay a heavy price for his goodness. And you, Mary, your hurt will be so profound, you will feel as though your heart was sliced through with a sharp sword."

For a while Simeon's words just hung there in the temple air. I was stunned, not believing what I had heard. Then slowly the devastating news came home to me: my son was going to be harmed. "Oh, no," I thought, "this cannot be!" All my joy drained out as fear and trepidation arose. I shook my head, trying to clear the faint feeling. My voice sounded hollow as I told Joseph I needed to sit down. "Terrible, terrible pain ahead for my child. Deep, deep heartache for myself." Over and over, those same chilling words whirled around in my head. What did it mean? Certainly future danger for my child, severe harm of some kind.

Joseph was alarmed, too. We were trying to compose ourselves when Anna, one of the temple widows, came by. She saw us sitting there, stunned and dismayed. She sat down beside me, gently took my hand in one of hers, and with the other she wiped the perspiration from my brow. Her face was that of one who had grown very close to God. There was such kindness and understanding in it. For months afterward I remembered the look on her face. As I began to feel at ease again, Anna took Jesus and rocked him gently. When she finally spoke, her words were filled with praise for the Holy One and gratitude for the birth of Jesus. She, too, promised that Jesus would make a great difference in people's lives.

Looking back now, I wish I had asked Simeon some questions and spent more time with Anna. But I was simply too dazed. Simeon had left us quickly after he spoke those terrifying words. Perhaps he, too, could not bear to think of what lay ahead for us. When we walked out of the temple, Joseph cradled Jesus protectively against his shoulder and held me close by his side. We left with such different feelings than those we had come with that day.

It took me quite a while to put Simeon's prophecy in perspective. I remember the day I felt peace slip fully inside of me again. I was washing dishes while Simeon's words churned inside my mind for the thousandth time. Suddenly I had this clear memory of the angel visiting me before Joseph and I were married. I remembered my struggle and confusion even though that message contained good news about the specialness of the child in my womb. I had so many questions at that time, and I had asked them all. The messenger kept telling me not to fear the future, assuring me that God would provide. I finally let go of my fears and doubts and said, "Yes, I will be honored to be an instrument of God. Let it be done."

It seemed to me that I had to find this hope again as I faced Simeon's prophecy. I had to go forward and trust the Holy One with my life no matter what sufferings might lie ahead. I had found the courage and faith to go through the difficult situations before Jesus' birth. Surely I would find this courage and faith again no matter what the future held. And so, once more I placed my confidence in the Holy One's promise to be an abiding source of strength for me.

Our "Simeons"

Our "Simeons" come upon us as unexpectedly as Mary's did. They come with equally harsh news and the inherent understanding that we will suffer in some way because of what has been announced to us. We don't want the news any more than Mary did. We don't deserve it any more than Mary did. But our Simeons appear anyway and with them come struggle and suffering.

Our Simeon prophecies usually enter our lives abruptly and without much warning. These announcements startle, shock, and confound us. They take us by surprise, wrench us out of our comfort zones, and blast us with their reality. The messages they carry bear promises of pain, grief, turmoil.

Many of us have experienced a "Simeon announcement" of some type. In the midst of a life that is going reasonably well comes the physician's prognosis of a serious illness or future surgery, the letter telling of a job ending, the family member sharing a shameful family secret hidden for years, the phone call speaking of death, the spouse declaring separation, the administrator announcing the closing of an institution or a major merger, the child insisting on a lifestyle in total contradiction to a parent's, a bank statement speaking for itself about a lack of finances.

I think of the parents who were told that their son had Down's Syndrome. They were shocked and found it very hard to believe, as no warning had been given before their child was born. Many fearful concerns instantly flashed through their minds, but, like Mary, they did not know how great their pain would be, only that the future would be difficult. Reflecting on their son's birth later in life, the mother said, "Little did I know at that time the pain and suffering I would go through over the years. It was hard enough to deal with his health problems, but it was even harder coping with his mental and emotional disabilities." I heard Mary's experience in this mother's story as she commented: "Even though I have gone through much sorrow and pain with Jerry, he has also been a source of great joy. I really believe he is a gift from God to us."

Sometimes our Simeons come from an internal rather than an external source. Our intuition and our night dreams are voices that can give us messages predicting future suffering. A woman named Debra had a dream that she thought was telling her about death. In her dream she saw her mom and grandma, who were still alive, with her dad, grandpa, and other relatives who had died years before. All these people were on the other side of the river waving to her. She had a strong sense that the dream meant that her mother and grandmother were going to die soon. She made a decision to spend more time with these two women and was thankful that she did because during that year they both died within three months of each other.

Another woman told me how she was teaching school when she was startled with the sudden thought, "I am going to hear that my father has died." She had no reason to think it and mentally gave herself a shake and admonished herself to pay attention to what she was teaching. That evening she had a phone call telling her that her father had been admitted to the hospital with pneumonia but that he would probably be released in a day or two. The following day he took a sudden turn for the worse. She hurried to reach the hospital, but he died before she arrived. Her inner prophecy had become a reality.

Our "Simeons" are a part of life. We cannot avoid them, try as we might. Likewise, we cannot plan for the kind of suffering and hurt that may await us in the future because of unwanted pronouncements. I have so often wished that I had been ready for surprising news that jolted me, but there was simply no way I could have foreseen what was coming. There have been numerous Simeons in my life, some of them bearing news of minor disasters and others large enough to mark my future with long stretches of pain.

I remember all too well the evening that I arrived at a hotel in Honolulu and the desk clerk handed me the small, square piece of white paper with the message: "Call home. Emergency." I doubt that he knew what a Simeon he was for me, but I knew the message meant that someone I treasured was in serious trouble. I didn't know until a phone call later that it was my father who had died of a heart attack. When I heard the heartbreaking news, I had no idea of how deep my sadness would be, but the overwhelming sorrow I immediately felt told me the future would hold much more of the same.

Responding to Our Simeons

The difficult and challenging messages, announcements, or revelations that we unexpectedly receive bring with them an immediate sense of concern and often alarm: Is this really true? What will happen now? How much hurt will there be? Can I get through this? What will I do? How can I handle this? What will become of me or of us? How long will this go on? How did this situation get to be this way?

When our Simeons bring us "bad news" we quickly become aware of how fleeting our peace and happiness is, how fragile our security, and how vulnerable our life can be. It is not unusual to initially experience fear, anger, disbelief, rage, intense sadness, emptiness, etc. All these responses are normal reactions to unwanted news. There is almost always a moment in our "bad news" time when we are stunned as Mary was. There is almost always a space in our life after startling, unwelcome news when we wonder whether our life will ever have peace and happiness again. We may want to lash out at the news and fight it. Eventually, we have to face the unwanted news, decide what our attitude toward it is going to be, and then deal with the situation as best we can. All of this takes time, love, and a tremendous amount of spiritual fortitude.

In the film *Good Will Hunting,* the wise therapist says to Bill, the young man who is hurting: "Bad things draw our attention to the good things we've overlooked." Mary didn't need Simeon's prophecy to convince her or remind her of what she had in the beauty and joy of her son. Mary already appreciated who and what she had in her life. But Simeon's words undoubtedly honed and sharpened her awareness of her son's presence and the goodness she found in many facets of her life.

When a life situation or event springs upon us and predicts future turmoil, what we value in life suddenly becomes sweeter, dearer, and more precious to us. For example, when faced with a prognosis of rheumatoid arthritis, mobility and pain-free days suddenly seem like a tremendous gift. When depression blankets our view of life with a deep void, the free and easy joy we assumed each day becomes something that we long for and relish.

Our Simeon messages are invitations to live each day gratefully and to enter each day fully. They can gift us with deeper awareness of how much we have taken for granted: our good health, our job, our home, our loved ones. When bad news jars our peace and crowds out our joy, it is a wake-up call: Attend! Notice! Look! Appreciate! Affirm! Beyond the shock of the bad news and its consequences comes the invitation to be grateful for what we simply assumed was ours for the keeping.

If, like Mary, we live in the fullness of each day, mindfully aware and grateful for that which brings us meaning, happiness, contentment, and security, we will not be spared the devastating emotions that spring up at a time of unwanted news, but we will also not be burdened with guilt or regrets over not having recognized and appreciated what is being taken from us.

The Gift of Anna

The Gospel of Luke describes Anna as being "of a great age, having lived with her husband seven years after her marriage, then as a widow to the age of eighty-four. She never left the temple but worshiped there with fasting and prayer night and day" (Luke 2:36–37). Think of it: Anna the aged woman and Mary the very young woman meeting at such a crucial time. How much Mary must have needed her. Anna's early widowhood had given her a fuller understanding of life. She knew what suffering was. Her many years in the temple deepened her relationship with God. She knew what surrender and fidelity meant. Anna came as a sign of hope and a source of strength for Mary. She came as a comfort to this young mother who had just learned that she would have much sorrow in the future.

I have always been struck by the scriptural detail which tells us that Anna "came by *just at that moment.*" Our "Annas" come when we need them. They come "just at the right time" in the form of a phone call, a letter, a person at the door, a compassionate nurse at a bedside. They may not say a lot to us, may not even realize how profoundly they are a messenger of hope to us. But we know...and we gain courage from their presence. They bring us a touch of comfort and hope as we embark upon a time of suffering. Our "Annas" are messengers from God. They are compassion-filled people who are not afraid to be with someone who is hurting. They are faith-filled people who bring us encouragement as much by their presence as through their words. They are hope-filled people who bless us by their constant certainty of our ability to overcome adversity.

My mother met her "Anna" several months after my father died. Like Anna, she came by "just at that moment" and blessed my mother's life in ways my mother never would have imagined. My mother's "Anna" came in the form of a neighbor named Wilda, who lived next door in the condominium where my mother moved after my father's death. Like Anna, Wilda had known hard times. She was prayerful, compassionate, and she understood my mother's sorrowful heart. Wilda became my mother's best friend, and she helped to bring her back to life.

Sometimes our "Annas" have no idea that they are helping us with the pain that follows a Simeon announcement. I recall the story of a grandmother named Jolene who told how stunned and worried she was when her unmarried Caucasian daughter phoned to say that she was pregnant with the child of an African American with whom she was no longer in relationship. Jolene's daughter had no money and needed a place to live. Jolene said her feelings went beyond immediate financial concerns to what it would be like to have a biracial grandchild. She was embarrassed for herself and worried for the child. She struggled with these feelings until the day when she was working at a pediatric clinic. On that day she was examining a two-month-old biracial child of a young couple. Jolene explained how her heart changed in that moment: "As their beautiful dark-skinned, brown-eyed boy's gaze locked on mine, I heard a voice telling me not to fear the events that were unfolding in my life. I understood I was being offered a gift. God would help me through all my trials." Several months after this, her grandchild was born, and Jolene quickly bonded with him.

She wrote: "I love this grandson deeply." (Who ever would have thought that a two-month-old child would be an "Anna" for a grandmother in pain over the news of a future grandchild?)

Our Simeons Force Us Deeper

When Mary heard Simeon's pronouncement, she was already living at a deeper level of life. Her struggle and her response at the time of the Annunciation indicate her depth of spiritual awareness. Mary's faith shone through as she accepted the Holy One's invitation to allow her womb to be a sacred vessel for Jesus. But Simeon's words forced her even deeper. She had to face the questions of "when" and "what if" and "how" all over again. Mary had to dip deeply into her reservoir of faith in order to move beyond the dread and fears that naturally arose. She had to stretch and reach again for the hand of God and believe that she could hold it tightly when her time of suffering came.

Our Simeon prophecies are often the first step of a journey that refines and purifies us, sets us in a certain direction, makes us stronger, sends us deeper. Down, down we go into unknown territory, into confusion, doubt, concern, worry, and uncertainty. Sometimes our Simeon experience stretches our confidence so thin that the fingertips of our faith can barely touch God. With the foretelling of future trials, we have to search for where our strength is and to trust that we will make it through whatever the future entails. It is a time when we are forced to ask the question: "Are you going to be with me in this, God?"

We never know ahead of time what our "Simeon prophecy" will mean for our lives or how it will draw us deeper. Matt told me what happened to him as a young man. One day a letter came in the mail with news he did not want to read: he had been drafted into the army at the time of the Vietnam war. Matt dreaded the thought of going, but on the advice of others he decided he must obey and do his part. During his training he was taught "about unimaginable and horrific things" that he might be expected to do to other people. Matt said he felt this was evil, and it led him to his chaplains to ask for a change in status; he told them he could not carry a weapon because it went against everything inside of him.

Matt's chaplains asked him "difficult questions about the just and unjust nature of war" which frustrated rather than helped him because he could not answer their questions. Matt said it was this that led him on a great search, "studying, studying, studying," researching the basis of every religion's beliefs. He sought answers to what people believed about God, life, war, and peace. His struggle took him deeper and deeper as he sought to know what all this meant. As Matt described it to me: "Being drafted was an immense spiritual struggle for me, but as a result, I learned so much about the world's religions, philosophy, theology, and spirituality." Matt survived the war that waged internally and externally and returned home a much wiser and spiritually stronger man because of it.

At the time of receiving a Simeon announcement it is almost impossible to know how it will affect our life. We have immediate concerns and thoughts about the future and what suffering we will have, but it is only in living out the process that we understand how it affects us. Likewise, we do not know what possible gifts it might bring to us. No matter how devastating the news might be, it can bring us an opportunity to grow spiritually. It is difficult to trust that this is true when we are face to face with painful news, but it is such a help if we do believe it.

Distressful news requires that we turn in faith and trust to the Holy One who is our root and foundation of love. This turning can ease the fear and panic that our Simeon announcements ignite. Mary had to gather her inner convictions, trust her relationship with God, and move ahead with the firm belief that God would neither abandon her nor let her worry and concern destroy her peace of mind. Mary did not know how the future would unfold any more than we do. Like Mary, we need to trust that God will teach us how to climb our mountain when the time comes and lead us to a place of peace.

I Speak to Mary

Mary, you have been there before me.
You have been dismayed and shocked by terrible, unwanted news.
You have known fear, sadness, and worry about the future.
You have had to quiet the heartaching distress within you.

You did not give up hope.
You did not drown in a pool of self-pity.
You did not let disappointment and anger
destroy your ability to love.
You placed your trust in God.

Woman of Compassion, Mother of Sorrows,
I draw inspiration from your journey.
I, too, can move through the pain of my present situation.
Your faith and courage lead me to my own.

Facing the Unknown

Kind and caring God,
my once secure life
now holds tremendous change.
Come into my turmoil
and quiet my anxiety.
Be there with the gifts
of your peace and guidance.

Let me not be overwhelmed
with fear of the unknown.
Grant me the ability
to face what awaits me.
Take my hand and assure me
that you will always be with me,
no matter what the future holds.

Hearing Difficult News

Divine Companion,
the harsh voice of reality
thrusts its dagger into my heart.
Statements and facts
I do not want to hear
get lodged in my memory
and scrambled in my mind

Help me not to panic.
I need to be patient
with what is before me,
to take one day at a time.
Grant me courage
to face the consequences
that may come from this situation.
May peace of mind and heart
soon return to me.

Fear of the Future

Guide and Protector,
Fear of the future gnaws at me.
Thoughts of what might happen
disrupt my equanimity.
I long to have a safe and secure life,
full of joy and well-being.

Help me to recognize my fears,
to see how they push me around
and shove me into deadening corners.
Do not let them have control over me.
Protect me from all those concerns
that threaten to overwhelm me
when I think about this situation.

I give myself and all my worries
into your wise and merciful care.
I entrust to your loving heart
my anxiety and my weariness.
You are near, guiding my life.
May this truth hold me fast.

Feeling Shock at the News

Faithful Shelter,
my life has suddenly changed.
I feel numb and unbelieving,
stunned and alarmed.
It does not seem possible that my life
could be so quickly turned upside down.

Comfort me, Abiding Companion.
Wait with me while I try to grasp the truth.
Slowly reveal to me what I need to accept.
As the layers of the days ahead unfold
keep me safe in the shelter of your love.
Abide with me, abide with me.

Walking with One Who Has Received Difficult News

Source of Strength,
there are many people in my world today
who are hearing difficult news.
They will need an anchor of strength
to keep them from being swept away
in their waves of worry and fear.
You can be this anchor of strength for them.

In particular, I pray for _____ .
There is no easy way through this time of turmoil.
May _____ remain open and confident of your guidance.
Help me to be a source of compassion and hope for her (him).

Guided Imagery (for one who is upset by painful news)

Begin by quieting yourself.

Take a deep breath. Let the breath out slowly. Do this three or four
   times.

Relax. Be at ease.

Remember that you are held in the arms of God's protective love.

Go inside. Feel the turbulence within you.

Let the doubts, questions, fears come to the surface.

Picture them as wild waves on the sea.

Now visualize yourself in a boat tossed on those wild waves.

Feel the tossing to and fro by the huge gusts of wind, the heaving,
   frothy waves. . . .

See the water of the gigantic waves slip over the edge of your boat.

Hear the roar of the storm. . . .

Turn and see Mary in the boat with you.

Visualize her sitting next to you, wrapping love around you.

Tell Mary what is most difficult for you. . . .

See how she understands, how she looks upon you with love.

Let this love envelop your being. . . .

Feel the wild waves gradually grow calmer.

Let their rhythm change from crashing and heaving

to a gentle rhythm of ebb and flow. . . .

Hear the wind quiet to a gentle breeze.

Sit peacefully in the boat of your life.

Now she speaks very tenderly to you:

"This is a difficult time for you.
Bring your fears and worries to the Holy One.
Your inner peace will return to you.
I understand the turmoil in your heart.
Your sorrow is my sorrow. You are not alone."

Let yourself be held in the arms of Mary's love. . . .
Let your fears, worries, concerns, slip away from you. . . .
Rest. Be at ease. . . .
Stay with Mary for a while and then thank Mary for being with you.
Bid her farewell and slowly come back to this time and place.

For Personal Reflection and/or Group Discussion

1. Reflect upon some of your past Simeon moments.

   Think of a painful announcement or news that you received.

   How did this affect your life?

2. How do you find yourself responding when you receive difficult news?

   What is your initial response? (anger, disbelief, sadness, silence, rage, self-pity, withdrawal, blaming...?)

   What have you found most helpful when you have received difficult news?

3. Have you ever had an "Anna" in your life?

   Have you had the opportunity to be an "Anna" for someone else?

4. Have you ever had to be a Simeon for someone else?

   Did this experience change you in any way?

5. Has your relationship with God influenced how you have experienced your Simeon moments? If so, how?

6. If Mary was sitting with you now, what would you want to say to her or ask her about this first sorrow in her life?

The Second Sorrow:
The Flight into Egypt

FLEEING FROM DESTRUCTION

"Get up, take the child and his mother, and flee to Egypt, and remain there until I tell you; for Herod is about to search for the child, to destroy him." (Matt. 2:13)

Mary Speaks

It must have been one or two o'clock in the morning when I felt Joseph's hand on my shoulder, urging me to wake up. I was startled and confused. We normally began our day with the first rays of morning light, but it was still very dark. "Mary, Mary, wake up," he called insistently. As I rolled over, I heard the heavy dread in his voice: "Mary, I've had a horrible dream." Usually I would not have been surprised that Joseph had a dream. He often did. It was one of the many things I loved about him. He would often turn to me in the morning and tell me about some dream of his that was either puzzling or delighting him. But that night it was different.

Joseph told me there was an angel in his dream, warning him to get up and take Jesus and me, to hurry into Egypt as fast as we could. The angel said that King Herod was jealous of our child and wanted to kill him. I tried to shake

51

the sleep out of my head. I just couldn't believe what I was hearing, so I asked Joseph to tell me the dream again. He was rarely impatient with me, but this time his voice grew firm and he repeated with alarm, "Mary! We have to go. Now!"

I knew Joseph would never frighten me like that unless he was deeply convinced of what he said. I struggled to grasp what was happening. Our child was in grave danger. I heard the concern in his voice. Suddenly terror seized my heart. The child, our child, was going to be killed! We must get ready immediately! Just that quickly, I had Simeon's prophecy on my mind again. "Oh, no," I gasped inside, is this what the holy man had foreseen? Is this when Jesus will be hurt? Will I lose him to Herod? I cannot begin to describe the fear that clutched at me.

There was so much to do and so little time. We wanted to leave before dawn so no one would see us go. I hurried to where Joseph was already tossing things together. Jesus began to cry, his little voice wailing, wanting attention. I picked him up and nursed him, holding him with one arm, while we hastily prepared to leave. First Joseph and I had to decide what we could carry with us. We didn't have much, but we quickly recognized many essentials had to be left behind — extra cloths for diapers and bedding, my special water jars and some of the less needed bags of herbs, the colorful, heavy blanket my mother had woven for me, and a lot of Joseph's favorite tools. They were too weighty for the long journey ahead of us. We needed to travel as lightly and freely as possible.

My mind was awhirl with what to take, trying to keep Jesus quiet, and gather what food we could. I sorted and Joseph packed. Soon we had arranged our bundles and were ready to set out. It was the time of a new moon so we did not have the luxury of moonlight to guide us, only the stars overhead. But the stars were brilliant. I looked up and found comfort in them. I always did. The Holy One seemed closer to me whenever the stars were shining. All those far-reaching lights seemed to say, "You are not alone."

I held Jesus close to me as we started out, Joseph and I both knowing and dreading what lay ahead of us. It would never have been a journey of our choice. We had felt settled and secure in our small home, and we had heard many stories of wild bandits on the roads who killed easily for simple trinkets. The terrain would be fiercely rugged, extremely dry in places, and it could be difficult to find enough food and water as we traveled the long passage to Egypt. But something deep inside told me Joseph was right. We had to go if we wanted to keep our son alive and safe.

It was a grueling journey. We kept to ourselves as much as possible so we would not have to answer questions. Joseph went without food more often than I did. He was always willing to do without so Jesus and I could have something. As we drew further and further away from our homeland I felt less and less secure. What would we do without a common language? Would we be accepted in a strange land? Would Jesus be safe there? Could Joseph find work to support us? There were many unknowns, and they scurried around in my mind like little desert creatures. Each day I turned my heart many times to the Creator and asked for freedom from the worries that attacked me.

We finally crossed the border into Egypt and found a place to settle. It was lonely and we found it challenging to adjust to the language and customs, but we would have endured anything to keep our beloved son from the destructive hands of Herod. By the time I had been accepted by the village women and developed several wonderful friendships, Joseph had another dream, this time about going home. So once more we packed up and moved on, trusting that we would be safe as we made the long journey home.

Our Flights into Egypt

Mary and Joseph's escape from Herod is similar to the flight of many people today from threatening situations that would bring them harm. The most obvious group of people are those who have been forced to leave their homelands because of political warfare, economic upheavals, religious and ethnic persecution, or devastating natural disasters such as earthquakes and famine. There are over thirty-seven million refugees on our earth today. Each refugee is a child, woman, or man who has left things behind that we easily take for granted: people who knew and loved them, a language with which to communicate, treasured possessions, and a place called "home."

Mary and Joseph's escape from Herod is also symbolic of our life. We, too, have our "Herods" that threaten to harm us. It was insecurity, jealousy, obsessive desire for power, and fear of the unknown that led Herod to destroy all that got in his way. There are situations when we know that if we continue to live with things as they are, they will be as destructive for us as Herod was in his time. Unless we change direction or leave the situation in order to save our physical, mental, emotional, or spiritual lives, we will pay a death-like price to some vital part of ourselves.

Our "flights into Egypt" are those times when destructive situations force us to take ourselves away from conditions that could bring us immense hurt or keep us from being the person we are meant to become. If we continue to perpetuate or stay in those situations, dreadful consequences will result. Our "Herods" can suffocate our dreams, erode our enthusiasm, damage our faith, ruin our health, or turn us into resentful, angry persons whose spirits are withered with unresolved conflict.

There are many kinds of "flights into Egypt" which people have to make every day. When a person with an addiction such as substance abuse, gambling, or obsessive shopping goes through treatment, he or she cannot afford to be around those who have remained in their addictive behavior. It is unsafe for them because they can easily be wooed back into old destructive patterns.

Sometimes our work situation demands that we flee by terminating stressful work situations that consume our physical health and invade the well-being of our family life. Or it may be that we will need to flee from destructive practices by confronting employers or employees who allow and promote racial and gender prejudice even if this means that we have to say goodbye to the peaceful working relationship we once had.

Hard as it is to acknowledge, there are also "Herods" in some churches. We may have to leave a religion, or a congregation, that has lost the essence of its spiritual inspiration and has become a source of inner death rather than spiritual life. We may have to flee physically by moving out of neighborhoods where crime and gangs terrorize and victimize the residents and hold them hostage with fear and threats. We may need to depart from a style of eating and drinking that encourages or enables heart disease or diabetes or other fatal illnesses. Our flight may involve discontinuing a relationship with someone whose unethical or immoral values greatly influence us and cause us to compromise our own values.

Our flight may be that of leaving the "Herod" of abuse. If we do not leave a destructive relationship it will wrap its vicious tentacles around us and squeeze the life out of our ability to love. There are people who will destroy us unless we remove ourselves from their presence. Constant, hostile verbal abuse belittles and shrivels self-esteem. Physical abuse batters and maims bodies. Sexual abuse obliterates the sacredness of love-making, destroys self-worth and a sense of personal goodness. When any of these destructive actions take over our lives there is a "Herod" in our midst. We have to make decisions about how we will save our lives.

Sometimes we need to flee from a part of our own self that creates a destructive or unhealthy pattern for us. We may need to leave behind a message that continually tells us we are no good, or a memory that always brings up resentment or harbors hatred, or a daydream that zaps all of our time and energy with sexual fantasies, or a silence about our sexual orientation when it kills our honesty and our integrity.

I remember vividly the woman minister who came to me with agonizing questions of how much longer she could keep her homosexuality hidden from her congregation. Her secrecy was eating the heart out of her enthusiasm for life. She feared rejection and possible loss of her church position if she revealed who she truly was. She finally took the great risk of speaking to her congregation about her sexual orientation. This woman minister received an amazing and gratifying response from those who listened to her. They welcomed her honesty and assured her of their acceptance of her. Although they did not all agree with her, they had come to know that her heart was centered on God and that was sufficient for them. Finally she was free of the "Herod" of secrecy that had pushed and cornered her so many times.

It may be an old grudge that becomes our "Herod." I recall a man who told me about his tremendous anger toward his father who had deliberately deceived him. After much counseling and spiritual guidance, the son knew that his anger had become his "Herod." It was destroying his peace of mind and influencing his attitude toward everyone. He knew that he needed to let his anger go and forgive his father. One day he said to me, "I don't want to let go of my anger. If I forgive my father, who will I have to blame?"

It is not always easy to leave what is harmful to us even though it is for our own good. We grow secure in what we have, even if it is damaging to us. There's always some fear of what we'll do or how we'll be or what others will think if we don't have this harmful habit or pattern. We can also hesitate leaving by muddling around in the question of whether it is the right thing to do or not.

Taking a stand for our own well-being and leaving a harmful situation can feel like a selfish thing to do even when we know that the person or situation is unhealthy for us. Vera told me how she had befriended the minister's wife at a time when this woman was lonely and friendless. As the year progressed, Vera discovered that this lonely woman had "a darker side." She used people; she wanted to be taken care of and demanded Vera's time constantly. According to Vera, "She was only interested in herself and how she could run everyone's life her way." When Vera went into a severe depression the following year this woman called her frequently to give her unsolicited advice, and Vera ended up feeling worse than ever. Vera said, "I realized that she was draining the tiny bit of energy I had. Now I try to stay clear of her because I realize that she always pulls me down. I feel selfish about this, but I do believe it is the right thing for me to do."

There are many inner messages that try to convince us to ignore the harm that is being done to us. As much as we might tell ourselves we want to flee from what hurts us, there is often an equally strong part of us that says, "Stick around. It can't be all that bad." Our rational minds can play tricks on us and try to deceive us, especially if we are feeling insecure. We may desperately need a job change because the stress is "killing" us, but the strong rational voice says, "This is stupid. You've worked long, hard years to get to this point. You will have no financial security if you leave." Our emotional world can also leap up and keep us from making good choices about a departure from old, harmful ways. We may need to leave a relationship, but guilt pulls at the heart and says, "Maybe I didn't try hard enough."

Joseph heard the message to flee from Herod in a dream. There are three of his dreams recorded in a few short verses of Scripture, dreams that led Joseph and Mary to make life-changing decisions. If we are relying only on our rational mind to tell us what to do we may never hear the message. If we let our emotions rule us, we may also never make the choice to leave. We may not even realize that we are in a Herod-like situation until we listen deeply to our intuition and inspirations, as well as to our night dreams. We do not always know on the surface of life what it is that intends to "do us in." And sometimes everything that is rational and logical tells us the wrong thing.

When to Stay and When to Flee?

The danger to our external or internal life can be so severe that we know immediately that it is time to flee. On the other hand, there are times when fleeing can take an immense amount of reflection, counseling, and inner struggle before a coherent decision to leave can be made. The phone rang one day when I was in the early stages of writing this chapter. A friend I'd not heard from in a long time called to let me know what was happening in her life. She told me that she was finally separating from her husband. They had tried and tried to work through their marital problems, but no amount of counseling or prayer had made a significant difference. Now he was having an affair. For many years she had given her entire energy trying to save their dying marriage. She realized that if she continued to do so, she would not have a life left to live.

Then she asked me about my work and what I was writing. When I described what I thought the flight into Egypt meant, she interrupted me and said, "Oh, that is exactly what I feel I am going through. I have to leave even though I want to stay. It's just too unhealthy for me to continue in this relationship that I have treasured for such a long time."

Sometimes it is better *not* to run or to flee from our "Herods." Sometimes we need to stay and "do battle" even at great risk to ourselves and to our loved ones. Sometimes we just have to "tough it out," "hang in there," and "ride the rough waters." We need to stay when we know that there is a reasonably good chance that things can change with confrontation, or counseling, or consistent efforts to alter behavior. We probably need to stay if we tend to run away quickly from anything that hurts. In our Western culture we run away from problems all too quickly because we have such a deep aversion to suffering.

We may also have to stick around when it seems as if the alternative to leaving would be even more destructive to us or to our loved ones. For example, a man may find the dying process of a spouse adding to his own health problems, but fidelity urges him to give his life to the loved one. A woman in a religious community may realize that fewer new entrants and a rapidly aging membership indicate the dying of the organization but still make a choice to stay because of love and commitment even though there is little that is intellectually or spiritually life-giving for her.

There are no easy answers of when to go and when to stay in a tough situation. One thing is certain: when we are in our "Herod" moments we must pray continually for guidance to know what to do. We will need wise ones to help us with our decision-making and choices. We will need objective people who can encourage us to take the steps we need in order to save our life or the life of our loved ones.

There is also the aspect of insecurity when it comes to fleeing our "Herods." When I first heard of women who were badly abused physically yet who kept going back to their abusive partners in spite of their broken bones and knocked-out teeth, I could not understand it. "How could anyone not leave a situation like that?" I thought. Then, when I had to face an experience of choosing to leave my work because the director of my work-place pressured and harassed me, I finally understood. Even though I had come to hate going to work and felt all my enthusiasm and energy dying, I didn't want to leave. I was angry about having to leave, but, equally, I was *scared* to leave. There was great security where I was, and I was fearful of what lay ahead even though I had been successful in my work.

Living with the Consequences of Fleeing

Fleeing from our "Herods" is one thing. Accepting the consequences is an-other. Mary and Joseph not only left in terror; they also journeyed into strange and alien territory. Things were not the same as they had been back home. The foreign land brought vulnerability and loneliness. It demanded time and energy to adjust. It took faith and trust that the future would be good to them. Yet, this discomfort and uneasiness was worth the price of keeping their son safe and free from harm.

When we flee from our "Herods," we are doing so in order to protect and guard our life. Whether this leave-taking is about our physical life or about our inner life, it is always a move toward greater freedom. On the spiritual path, inner freedom is essential for growth. Often there is a price to be paid for this movement away from what keeps us from being fully alive human beings. There are consequences to being more whole that we would much rather not accept. Our "flights" can take us into "strange lands" for a while. We may have to adapt our style of living or our way of relating to others. We may have to search intently for a way to be at home with our new self. It takes a lot of courage to forge ahead into unknown territory and leave our secure land behind.

We never know what the price for our freedom will be until we have taken the step away from our "Herod" and toward our new land. It took a tremendous amount of fortitude for a woman named Lacy to admit that she had been sexually abused by her brother and his friend when she was very young. This Herod-like experience had hung in the closet of her memory for many years. She wrote: "The decision to face my past history took every ounce of strength and courage I had." Her flight to a new land cost her dearly. When she finally sought help to heal from the hurt, her family and religious community both refused to give her support and understanding. The consequences for Lacy were loneliness and a feeling of rejection by those she had counted on to be there for her. The greatest thing she left behind, in her words, was the religious community that refused to accept her process and asked for her dismissal. In spite of these painful consequences Lacy did eventually find much inner freedom. As Lacy summarized it: "I am grateful for the skilled therapist who untangled many issues and for a gracious God who did not abandon me."

Whenever we are fleeing from dangerous and destructive people and situations, we will need to pray for daily guidance, confront our fears, be willing to be insecure for a while, and find wise persons to help us listen to our truest selves. It is comforting when we are fleeing our "Herods" to remember the journey that Mary took. She, too, walked into unknown terrain in order to find freedom and safety. She, too, faced her fears and accepted the consequences of leaving a harmful situation. She, too, turned to the Holy One as a source of strength and sustenance. Mary has been there before us. She was given the inner gifts she needed for the unknown journey. We will also be given what we need. We are not alone.

I Speak to Mary

Mary, you have been there before me.
You have had to leave what was harmful
for you and your loved one.
You have known how difficult it is to move away.
You have experienced the consequences.

You trusted the guidance of God through Joseph.
You listened to the deepest part of yourself.
You bravely walked into unknown territory.
You willingly gave up a life you knew
so that your child would be safe.
You did not let anxiety and fear keep you
from doing what you had to do.

Woman of Compassion, Mother of Sorrows,
I draw inspiration from your journey.
I, too, can move through the pain of my present situation.
Your faith and courage lead me to my own.

Seeking Refuge

Loving Refuge,
I am on the lonely road,
trying to find my way.
I need your protection
to keep me from harm.
Gather me under your wings.
Embrace me with your compassion.
Comfort me in my uncomfortableness.
Rest me in the caress of your enduring love.

Sheltering One,
I draw near to you,
confident that you will be my home
when all other homes are lost to me.

Moving Away from the Known

Divine Journeyer,
I am in a strange, unsettling place
in my transitory life.
I have left much behind me.
I have questions about the changes
and wonder about the adjustments.
It is easy to doubt my decisions
and to wonder if I will be all right.

Assure me of your nearness.
Clothe me in a garment of hope.
Teach me to be patient
as I find my way in life.

Seeking Guidance

Far-Seeing One,
this change in my life
is very difficult for me.
The familiar patterns
of my world
are tossed askew.
The strongholds
and insecurities
that gave me control
are unraveling.
It is time to let go.

It is time to trust
that you know the way.
It is time to allow you
to be my guide.

Vulnerability

Faithful Protector,
I feel vulnerable.
I am easy prey
for those who can hurt me.

Teach me how to protect myself
without building walls
that keep me from needed growth.
Help me to have good boundaries.
Shield me from harm.

Draw me away
from what can destroy me.
Lead me toward
what will encourage my gifts.
May I become
an ever more loving person.

Walking with One Who Needs to Flee

Source of Peace,
there are many people in my world
who live in dangerous or hurtful situations.
They need courage to leave.
They need safety and protection.
You can be the peace they seek.
You can be the shelter they need
as they let go and move on with their lives.

In particular, I pray for _____
as I encourage her (him) to flee from harm.
Be a strong ally and a comforting refuge for her (him).
Guide and direct _____ to a place of freedom and growth.

Guided Imagery (for one who needs to flee from harm)

Begin by quieting yourself.

Take a deep breath. Let the breath out slowly. Do this three or four
  times.

Relax. Be at ease.

Remember that you are held in the arms of God's protective love.

Go inside to a place that feels safe and secure.

Sit down in that place of refuge and comfort.

Recall the difficult situation of your life.

See as clearly as you can what is harmful for you. . . .

Now see Mary coming to you.

She looks at you with great kindness.

Invite her to sit beside you. . . .

She holds her hand out to you and you put your hand in hers.

Feel the safety and comfort of her hand.

Notice how strong her hand is, how welcoming. . . .

Talk to Mary about your difficult situation.

Tell Mary what you find especially hard about leaving. . . .

Listen to Mary as she tells you how to find strength and courage to
  leave. . . .

Feel the power of Mary's presence. . . .

Let this strength enter into your heart.

Notice how it fills you with courage to do what you need to do. . . .

The two of you now stand up. Mary blesses you.

She whispers gently to you:

"You need to be free from harm.
Take courage and leave what has the power to harm you.
Do not lose heart. You can be free.
I understand your struggle.
Your sorrow is my sorrow. You are not alone."

Stay with Mary for a while and then thank Mary for being with you. Bid her farewell and slowly come back to this time and place.

For Personal Reflection and/or Group Discussion

1. What do you think is most difficult about being forced to "flee" in order to be safe from harm?

2. How would you try to help a person who was being hurt because someone or something was being destructive for him or her?

3. Have you ever experienced a "Herod" in your life?

   (Have you ever left someone or something that was harmful for you?)

   If so, describe how this happened for you.

4. What is most helpful spiritually when you are in a situation that requires a difficult moving on?

5. Has your relationship with God influenced how you have experienced leaving something or someone harmful? If so, how?

6. If Mary was sitting with you now, what would you want to say to her or ask her about this second sorrow in her life?

The Third Sorrow:
The Loss of the Child Jesus in the Temple

SEARCHING FOR
OUR LOST TREASURES

When the festival was ended and they started to return, the boy Jesus stayed behind in Jerusalem, but his parents did not know it. Assuming that he was in the group of travelers, they went a day's journey. Then they started to look for him among their relatives and friends. When they did not find him, they returned to Jerusalem to search for him.

(Luke 2:43–45)

Mary Speaks

Those were good years for us once we settled in Nazareth and were able to leave behind the horrible experience of running from Herod. Joseph became well known for his carpentry, and I was able to resume my bread baking, selling it each day in the marketplace. All the while we both enjoyed Jesus. He was an easy child to raise. I certainly never expected the challenge that awaited me when he was twelve. That year we made our usual family trip to Jerusalem to celebrate the festival of Passover. We always enjoyed the hustle and bustle of the

71

city, the beautiful rituals in the temple, and the gathering of friends and relatives. When we left to return home the roads were again crowded with throngs of pilgrims like ourselves.

That particular morning Jesus had started out walking with me but then he soon disappeared. I supposed he had gone to travel with the men's group. It was only in the evening when Joseph and I met for our meal that we took alarm. Jesus rarely missed a meal. Like all boys his age, he loved to eat. At first I said nothing, assuming Jesus was with our relatives and friends, but when the meal was ready and the sun had begun to set, Jesus still had not joined us. I turned to Joseph and said, "When did Jesus leave your group today?" Joseph looked surprised, saying: "Jesus was never in our group. I thought he spent the day with you."

The first sharp edge of fear poked at my heart. Where was he? Joseph calmed me by suggesting that he was surely with our relatives or friends. We left our meal and went hurriedly to check with them. Each group had discouraging news for us. No one had seen Jesus all day. I realized, then, that Jesus was lost, or hurt, or even worse, maybe apprehended, lured and caught to be sold as a slave or a pawn of men. Panic seized me. I began calling his name, running everywhere, interrupting people's meals, asking them about Jesus. No one could recall seeing him.

It was late by the time Joseph and I realized we had to retrace our steps back to Jerusalem. I was shaking with fear as we repacked, praying all the time to the One who had been with me in other fearful times. It was a starless night with thick clouds overhead as we headed back in the bleak darkness. Over and over I prayed for our son's safety and for someone to lead us to him. Along the way we stopped to wake travelers, to ask about Jesus. People were tired and some were gruff and sharp with us. They told us we ought to take better care of our son.

As we continued back to the city, my fears and apprehensions grew deeper and stronger. Day dawned and I looked at Joseph. His eyes were dark pools of sadness and concern. Neither of us spoke. Sorrow weighed heavily on us. We *knew we had to put all our energy into finding our lost treasure. We reached the city in mid-afternoon, exhausted and deeply worried. Where would we begin to look? We started on the west side and found it a grueling effort. It seemed an impossible task; so many boys were Jesus' age. Would we knock on every door? Go through every marketplace? Would we find any clues at all about his disappearance? I kept crying out to the Holy One to guide us. I could not bear the thought of losing my child forever.*

Finally, we could do no more searching that day. It was too late and we were both completely drained. We lay down, exhausted, finding a small space on the side of an inn. We had neither eaten nor washed the whole night and day. We prayed together and asked for guidance. Both of us talked, then, about how guilty we felt: if only we had been more aware, more alert; if only we had been clearer with Jesus about traveling with us; if only we had warned him more about the dangers. We both encouraged each other to trust that the Holy One would help us find Jesus. We had known God's guidance before. We could not doubt now, even though our hearts wavered and felt great fear.

In spite of my desire to trust, I tossed and turned throughout the night. The next morning when we rose a chill was in the predawn air. We found some water and I noticed how wonderfully refreshing it felt on my tired face and swollen eyes. As the streets came alive, we tediously pushed our way through the crowds, describing our son again and again, asking if anyone had seen him. It was late that morning when an elderly woman selling baskets told us she had been over near the temple area the day before and that she might have seen a boy of his description there.

The temple! Of course! Why hadn't we thought of that before? Jesus was interested in everything that took place there. After what seemed forever, we neared the temple area. We stopped to catch our breath. Now what? I was full of hope and apprehension at the same time. We had just turned a corner in the temple when we both gasped. There was our twelve-year-old son, sitting among the learned rabbis, and he was speaking to them! They seemed rapt in attention. How could this be?

Tremendous relief swept through my heart in that moment. At the same time, I was angry with him. How could he do such a thing to us? Joseph and I walked up to the group, and it was then that Jesus noticed us. I couldn't help it. Even with all those rabbis present, I blurted out: "Son, why have you treated us like this? Do you know what we have gone through looking for you?"

And then more hurt came. Jesus didn't come immediately to us and tell us he was sorry. He looked at us with mild surprise and said the strangest thing: "Why were you looking for me? Didn't you know that I must be in my Father's house?" What did he mean? What was he trying to tell us? Joseph was confused, too. I could tell by his silence. I looked at Jesus, the son I loved so dearly and who was such a good child, and with all the strength I could conjure up, I said, "Son, it is time for you to come home with us."

To my great relief, he got up then and came over to us, giving us each a loving smile and embrace. I knew it was his young way of wanting us to understand and forgive him. I was too relieved to say anything except, "I love you." And then I cried. Later, when we had returned to Nazareth, I turned those three days and my son's response over and over again in my heart. It was such a mystery to me. Who was this child and who would he become?

Searching for Our Lost Treasures

If you have ever lost someone or something dear to you, if you have ever searched frantically for a lost beloved, or a missing part of yourself, you have been there with Mary in her search for Jesus. If you were seized by fear and dread, wondering if you would ever find what you had lost, you have entered into the third sorrow of Mary. If you have felt guilt, doubt, or anger, you know Mary's struggle of searching for Jesus. It is the sorrow of all those who lose and then search desperately for the pearl of their life that they once had and cannot find.

Although this third sorrow of Mary is like many types of loss, parents who have lost a child of any age, young or adult, can most identify with Mary's search. This child may be lost through drugs, prostitution, street gangs, or cults. This child may have intentionally left home. This child may have been lured, or snatched away without consent. Sometimes the child may be physically present but is "lost" to the parent because of family disagreements, hostile misunderstandings, and nonacceptance. The parents wonder "where" the child is because of his or her insistent silence and lack of communication.

I know of many parents who have lost their children. Mia's son got lost in drugs, and even when he does return home for family gatherings, he is never "there" because his heavy drug usage has damaged his brain and deadened his ability to relate well with others. Fred and Ann's daughter has been hospitalized numerous times for mental illness. Each time after her hospital stay they bring her home with them as she continues in her recovery program. She gets better for a while, but before long, she is lost again in the chaos of her mind and they lose their daughter once more. Anthony's adult son is lost to him because his son flew into a rage about family inheritances and left the house in a huff after a brief visit. Anthony has not heard from his son in three years.

Angeline and Patricia, two mothers who were at a retreat on transitions and grief, told me that each of them has a teenage daughter who has been missing for two years. Their daughters took up with gangs and went to live with them on the streets. These two distraught mothers have searched relentlessly for their young daughters, but they do not know where they are, or how they are, or if they are alive. Jose and Alicia's little boy was walking home from school one day. He never came home, and no one has ever discovered if this beloved one of their hearts is alive or dead. They have spent twelve heartbreaking years searching for some trace of their son.

There are parents in many countries, particularly in Central and South America, whose sons and daughters have "disappeared." In these places where there has been much political and religious upheaval, their children have often been forced out of their homes by brutal and vicious torturers. These children are victims of violent revolutions and harsh dictatorships. Out of their pain, parent groups such as "mothers of the disappeared" have been formed. They have gathered strength in their search by uniting in their outrage and their grief. The pain and determination of these parents to find their missing children echoes the pain and determination of Mary to find her missing child.

It is not just children who get lost. We can also lose adults in our lives through relational conflicts and other sources of departure and separation. There are times when we lose a partner or a good friend who may have been a part of our life for a long time. We search for what went wrong and how to repair the break. Sometimes our searching brings our friend back, and other times no matter how much effort we give to mending the differences, the relationship just doesn't fit anymore.

Sometimes the person we lose is our self. Some part of who we are and what we value can be hidden or unconsciously left behind for a time. We can lose things like our sense of direction in life, our identity, or the role that has shaped our persona. We can lose the part of us that holds hope for the future. We can lose our ability to cope or to function well under stress. It can be terrifying to lose our self.

A thirty-four-year-old woman told me the story of her husband walking out on her, leaving her with five young children. He left her with no money and no job outside the home to support herself. She was humiliated by having to rely on food stamps and exhausted by the pressure of job-hunting and being constantly concerned about her children who were "acting out" in school because of their own hurt over the loss. She said there were months when she hardly knew where she was, but she struggled on, trying to find a new life for her children and to figure out who she was and what she should do. For several years she often fell into near-despair, but eventually she found a good job and developed a life that held hope for herself and her five children.

It doesn't always have to be a jarring event that causes us to lose our self. Janice wrote and told me that she easily finds herself in the third sorrow of Mary because, in her words, "for most of my last thirty years, I have been searching for something that seems to be missing in my life. I used to label it 'wisdom,' 'truth,' 'enlightenment.' Now I know that it is a missing part of myself that I search for. This missing part, buried deep inside of me, is so elusive that I still have trouble believing it is there."

Retired people, especially early retirees, have told me that they have been surprised by how lost they felt after they left their workplace. They had so identified themselves with what they did that they were uncomfortable without the external identification of their position at work. As much as they might have wanted to have the freedom of not going to work, it took some time before they stopped feeling lost and began enjoying another lifestyle.

Like Mary's experience with Jesus, we don't always notice right away that these inner treasures are missing. There was a time when I lost my enthusiasm for my work. It was a gradual sort of thing, and I didn't notice that it was gone until the day I was sitting in front of my computer and I heard myself saying the word "hate." It was then that I noticed how I had been saying that word about everything: "I *hate* this pile of papers on my desk. I *hate* this thesaurus program on my computer. I *hate* preparing for talks, I *hate* deadlines, etc." I couldn't believe the passion with which I was saying the word "hate." When did my enjoyment of my work leave me, I wondered.

This awareness of my "hate" jolted me and led me to explore where I might have left my joy and satisfaction. I searched my motivation for ministry and reviewed my decisions about what I had chosen to do with my current schedule. It didn't take long to realize I had simply taken on way too much and was overly stressed. It was my own fault. No one else had caused it to happen. I was humbled to have heard the word "hate" in me, but gradually I found my enthusiasm again. It was a painful but good experience, helping me to be much more careful about what I choose to do with my time and energy.

The lost child in the temple can symbolize whatever and whoever we greatly treasure when we no longer have it in our possession: lost faith, lost good health, lost belief in self, lost happiness, lost financial security, lost values, lost peace of mind. We can lose so many things that we value and spend much time and energy in trying to regain them. It is as though we turn our back for a moment to attend to the incessant details of our lives, and when we turn around we learn, to our great dismay, that one of our very significant treasures has disappeared.

The Tension and Turmoil of Searching and Finding

Did Mary continue to feel irritated with Jesus? Was his behavior something that she had to struggle with for a while? Scripture does not indicate what

Mary thought and felt after they went home, only that Mary continued to reflect about all that had happened. Some scriptural translations say Mary "pondered" what had occurred while others say she "treasured" it in her heart. Mary had much to ponder. Most of us do when we spend time in a frantic, fearful search for someone or something that is a central part of our life. Mary's question to Jesus, "Why have you done this to us?" certainly has a tone of parental irritation and concern in it. As happy as we are to find our treasure, we may still have to deal with emotions like anger, confusion, and guilt that surfaced while we were searching.

Parents whose children betray their trust will have to come to terms with how to give this trust to their children again. A single parent told me the story of her teenage daughter who ran away from home while she was visiting her father. The daughter did not return for twelve excruciating days. The mother suffered fiercely not only from fear of what might happen to her daughter but also from the hostile treatment she received from one of the police officers when she brought photos and fingerprints of her daughter to the police station.

When the daughter finally returned home, the mother was tremendously relieved, but ever since that experience she always withheld a bit of her love from her daughter, feeling a vulnerable place inside for all the hurt and pain the daughter had caused her. She told me: "That experience was so painful for me. I searched for and found my daughter, but I never fully let her come back into my life. It was five years after that incident when I realized what had happened inside of me, how I was keeping some of my love away from her for fear she'd hurt me again. It was only then that I could finally welcome my daughter home fully, without any hesitations in my heart."

We need to forgive others and ourselves for the pain we had when we searched for our missing treasure. I met a respiratory care nurse who wept and wept as she described what happened when she was on duty in a neonatal ICU. She loved her work and was involved in caring for a three-month-old infant who was on life support. The baby died while in her care. She was accused of having set the ventilator humidifier incorrectly, thus causing the child's death. She told me that it was an intricate, complex system, and she thought that she had done the right thing with the machine. She lost her job because of the infant's death and was unable to be licensed anywhere. She had tried other work but ten years later still had not found peace. "I have worked and worked and worked with therapists. I have tried and tried and tried to get my life back. I am still trying," she sobbed. I felt her pain. I also sensed that one of the missing pieces of recovering her lost life was forgiveness. She needed to stop blaming her accusers before she would find peace, and she also needed to forgive herself.

Obsessive thinking and feeling can be huge boulders of tension as we search for and find what we have lost. We can spend a lot of wasted energy on "if only . . . " and "what if . . . " and "did I . . . ?" Whether our loss is intentional or accidental, many torturing questions arise: Whose fault is it? Is there someone I can blame? Why did it happen? Did I do enough or too much? Maybe I should have done this or said this. Why did I say that? On and on the questions come spilling into our mind. Guilt often jumps on our back when we are searching for someone or something we love. We can easily obsess about our part in causing the loss even when we know rationally that we did nothing wrong or that we intended to do the right thing even though it might not have been the best thing to do.

I was reminded of this at a retreat when Deirdre and I were discussing issues related to cancer. In the conversation, she told me that her daughter-in-law called one morning a few months earlier and said that Tom, Deirdre's son, was having medical tests to see if he had cancer of the tongue. Deirdre said she felt her heart fall out of her at these words, and she was filled with an immense dread of losing her son. No sooner had she gotten in touch with this fear than all sorts of guilty thoughts invaded her mental space. He smoked a lot and she wondered if she had breast-fed him right or fed him enough when he was young. Maybe that's why he smoked too much. She began obsessing over other things she had done, or not done, that might have caused his cancer. "It was difficult to stop these thoughts from pouncing on me, even though I knew that I was not to blame," she explained.

Living with Mystery

When they finally located Jesus, Mary did not understand what it meant. She was left to live with the mystery of what had taken place. Her child was found, but she did not comprehend why he had chosen to be hidden from her. She pondered this life experience, reflected upon it, turned it over in her heart again and again. Oftentimes parents do not understand, either, why children do what they do, why they choose values radically opposed to their own, why they respond as they do. Many times parents do not know why life has dealt them such a blow in the daughter who is missing or son who has died.

Sometimes we cannot figure out, either, why we have lost some part of our self that we have cherished and have had to painstakingly recover. Even after we stand in the temple of our soul and say, "Ah, there you are!" sometimes we still do not understand why our depression was so lengthy, why our spiritual energy waned into hopelessness, why our enthusiasm faded into lethargy. We may not know the answers for why things happened the way they did for many years, and perhaps we may never fully understand the "why."

There are circumstances when no amount of talking, healing therapy, good books to read, quiet reflection, intense research, or other deliberate searching adequately solves the story of "why." Sometimes we can sit for years inside the experience of losing a treasure and not have the satisfaction of knowing "why" it happened. We can grind and grind our rational teeth, trying to figure out what went wrong and the reason for it. We can spend our energy blaming ourselves or others for what took place, or we can forgive whoever and whatever caused our great search and then move on with our lives. There may always be a piece of mystery that is left to sit in our soul, to tug at us from time to time and keep us humbled by our inability to sort it all out.

Like Mary who pondered what she had lost and found, we also need to stand in the middle of the mystery of our life and reflect upon the message it has for us. By reflecting on our experiences, we can learn from them. Instead of just going busily about our life, we can let our inner eye scan our lost and found event and see what the deeper message might be for us. Once we have paid full attention to our experience, with all its hurt and turmoil, there comes a time when we must put the matter to rest even if we do not understand why this happened to us.

When we have lost a treasure and are searching for its return, it is time to reenter the temple of our soul. We ought never to go searching all alone. It is essential to call on God for guidance and direction. In our frantic, heartaching, panicky search for our treasure, we need a deep center of peace and harmony. This can be nearly impossible to feel when we are in the midst of a painful search. Yet, we must constantly give ourselves to divine peace, begging that we receive this peace so that we can search with a heart of love and trust.

I Speak to Mary

Mary, you have been there before me.
You were faced with things you did not understand.
You turned to God in your distress
and pondered your experience in your heart.
I have also encountered the realm of mystery.
I, too, do not understand.
I will also turn and ponder this in my heart.

Mary, you searched for your beloved child.
You experienced the distress and longing,
the agony of not knowing where he was.
I, too, search and wonder where my treasure is.
I am also longing to find my pearl of great price.
When will I find what I am seeking?

Woman of Compassion, Mother of Sorrows,
I draw inspiration from your journey.
I, too, can move through the pain of my present situation.
Your faith and courage lead me to my own.

Searching for Our Self

Good Shepherd, who finds the lost one,
the "me" I have known has disappeared.
Will I ever recover the person I have been?
Will I find who I am, and who I am becoming?

Protect me in this great vulnerability.
Assure me that I will come home to myself
even though my "self" may be different.
Silence my impatience. Calm my worry.
Restore my joy. Dispel my negativity.
Help me to befriend my new self with hope.

Searching for a Lost Treasure

Jesus, you told hope-filled stories
of lost treasures being found.
I am experiencing a great loss.
My searching seems futile.
My self-confidence feels frail.
I need to trust that I will find
what has been lost to me.
I need keen spiritual eyes.
Keep reminding me of lost coins
being recovered,
and pearls of great price being found.

Spirit of Guidance,
lead me.

Direct me so that I will discover
what is best for me to be and to do.
Above all, may my searching
lead me home to you.

Panic and Anxiety

Source of tranquillity,
be a peaceful presence for me.
Calm and settle my anxious spirit.
Set me free from my turmoil and fear.
Give me a perspective on my life.
Help me to trust that all shall be well.
Loosen my grip on my need to control.
May I live in this moment, now,
instead of looking into the vast journey ahead.
You are here, Peaceful One, you are here.
I rest in you.

Self-Blame and Guilt

Guiding Spirit,
free me of the mental and emotional assaults
that pound me with guilt and self-doubt.
I want to be honest with you and with myself.
Grant me clearness of mind and heart
so I can see and accept what is my fault
and let go of all that is not of my doing.

Forgive me for my deliberate failings
and help me to forgive myself.
Free me of all false messages
of guilt and blame.
May I love and accept myself
as warmly as you love and accept me.

Walking with One Who Is Searching

Compassionate God,
there are many people in my world
who are searching for something or someone they treasure.
There are parents filled with heartache for their lost child.
There are distressed persons searching for their very self.
There are countless grieving ones who are looking
for a piece of their life that once gave them happiness.

I am walking with _____, who is involved in a great search.
I want to understand and be with the distress of searching,
the anxiety of losing, the fear of not finding.
May I be a source of comfort, hope, and courage
while she (he) searches for what needs to be found.
May I be patient with the length of time it takes
and not hurry or push the process.
Bless all who are searching for lost treasure,
especially _____ .
May they turn to you often
and draw comfort from your guiding presence.

Guided Imagery (for one who is searching)

Begin by quieting your self.

Take a deep breath. Let the breath out slowly. Do this three or four
times.

Relax. Be at ease.

Remember that you are held in the arms of God's protective love.

Go inside.

Visualize yourself in a comfortable place where you can reflect on
your life.

Let yourself be at peace in this place....

Mary comes to be with you. Notice her clear eyes, her open presence.

She understands your search.

She knows how much you need hope and peace.

Feel her quiet and calmness.

Let it ease into your spirit....

Tell Mary about what you have lost, why this search is so vital to
you....

Listen to Mary's response to your experience of searching....

Ask Mary any questions you have....

Be at peace with this woman who knows your struggle....

Mary slips her hand into the pocket of her cloak.

She brings something out of it and asks you to hold out your hand.

Mary places a large, round pearl in your open hand.

Feel its roundness, how smooth it is.

Notice how beautiful the pearl is, how silky and white....

Mary speaks to you. She says:

"I give this pearl to you as a sign of hope.
Hold it as a trust that you will find what you need for your life,
I know what it is like to look and look for what you have lost.
Your sorrow is my sorrow. You are not alone."

Stay with Mary for a while and then thank Mary for being with you.
Bid her farewell and slowly come back to this time and place.

For Personal Reflection and/or Group Discussion

1. Have you had an experience in your life when you have lost someone or something of great value?

   If yes, what was this like for you?

   What kinds of thoughts and feelings did you have?

   How responsible did you feel for the loss?

   Did you recover your lost treasure?

2. What is the most difficult part of losing someone or something of great value?

3. What is most needed or most helpful for you when searching for a lost treasure?

4. Have you journeyed with someone else who was searching for a significant part of his or her life? If you have, what did you learn from this experience?

5. Has your relationship with God influenced how you have searched for the missing parts of your life?

   If so, how?

6. If Mary was sitting with you now, what would you want to say to her or ask her about this third sorrow in her life?

The Fourth Sorrow:
Mary Meets Jesus Carrying His Cross

MEETING OUR PAIN

A great number of the people followed him, and among them were women who were beating their breasts and wailing for him. (Luke 23:27)

Mary Speaks

I heard a frantic rapping on the door. My neighbor had come running to my house. She gasped for breath as she blurted out, "Mary, I've just heard — they've arrested Jesus in Jerusalem, accused him of some sort of criminal activity. I am so sorry to tell you this." I dropped the plate I was holding. My heart went numb before the plate shattered on the floor.

I shouldn't have been so shocked, I suppose. Jesus had been causing a stir ever since he left Nazareth to preach. Yet, I never thought it would come to this. I just couldn't believe that he would be arrested for his beliefs and activity. What would I do? My neighbor put her arms around me. She was such a dear one, that Rebecca. We had been good friends for a long time. She knew me well. "I'll go home and ask David if he will accompany us," she said, read-

91

ing my thoughts as only another mother could. She knew I wanted, needed, to see my son, and as a widow I could not travel alone that long distance to the city.

All the way to Jerusalem I prayed that the authorities would see the truth about my son and admit that he was no more a criminal than I was. Jesus had a soft heart for anyone in need. Kindness seemed to keep growing in him. I knew he spoke out against some of the religious laws and that he did not keep all of them, but he had never hurt anyone, of that I was sure. I prayed for Jesus, that he would be able to endure whatever was happening to him. There were such dreadful stories being circulated of the cruelty of those who imposed the Roman law on Jewish residents.

Surely they would come to know the good Jesus had done and dismiss his case. Yet, all the while I prayed with hope, another part of my heart sank into numb ache. I had not forgotten my encounter with Simeon over thirty years ago. I thought that the worst was yet to come. I always wondered when it would happen. "Oh," I whispered inside, "not now, not this way."

By the time we finally reached the gate of the city, I was dusty, weary, and worn out. We went immediately to the home of my cousin who lived not far from there. I thought he might know what had happened to Jesus. The streets were strangely empty and in the far distance we kept hearing a great commotion. My cousin and his wife were not at home. I grew more concerned. Perhaps they had gone to where Jesus was being held prisoner. We left our belongings and walked as quickly as our sore, long-journeyed bodies would go. The noise grew louder. It came from the heart of the city.

We had gone but a short distance when the streets began teeming with people. They were everywhere, pushing and shoving. I heard shouts of "There he is, over there!" We were caught up, then, in the press of the mob. It was impossible to turn back. I thought to myself, "How will we ever find where my son is being held?" I looked around and David and Rebecca were no longer with me, shoved back somewhere into the crowd. My heart grew faint. What could I do?

Just then the mob was pushed aside by the Roman soldiers. Down the street I saw what I had only heard about before: the forcing of criminals to carry their own pieces of wood on which they would later be crucified. I did not want to look at such degradation. No matter what a man had done, he did not deserve such horrible treatment. I saw in that quick glimpse from a distance that the piece of wood was too heavy for him to carry. He was bent over and walking with great pain.

As I stood there, hemmed in by the screaming mob, many were crying out, "Crucify him! Crucify him!" I heard the wailing of women following the man condemned to die. I knew that wailing all too well from the deaths in my own village, especially when Joseph had died. Suddenly a woman in front of me fainted. I was bending down to help her when the man carrying the wood drew so close that I could not help but look up into his face.

In one shuddering gasp, I saw my son! I took in the horror of his pain, the thorns pushed into his head, the deep gashes on the back of his neck that told me he had been scourged. It was only by the strength of God that I did not collapse. I rose up and it was then that Jesus saw me. Our eyes met and in that instant I felt all of his pain as if it was my own. It was a moment I shall remember all my life. It is as fresh and pain-filled as if it had happened today.

I thought that my heart would fall out of me. "My son! My son!" I cried. The soldiers pushed me aside and prodded him to keep moving. I cried out that I would gladly take his place, but my words were lost in the crowd. Finally I knew the sword that Simeon had prophesied. The pain of my son seared my heart. I knew that I would do anything to stay close to him. I edged my way in behind him and joined the women who were wailing. From the depths of my *soul came sounds I never knew existed. I wailed and I wailed as I walked in the suffering footsteps of my son.*

The Road of Suffering

One of the toughest things in life is to walk the journey of intense suffering of someone who is dear to us. Mary knew this when she encountered the tattered remnant of her child on the road to his death. When did Mary first meet Jesus on his final journey? We do not know for certain where she was when her son carried his cross to the site of his crucifixion. There is no specific mention of where they first met on that final path of suffering. The Gospel accounts tell us only that Mary was there at Golgotha ("the place of a skull"), standing beneath his cross.

Legend has long held that at some moment Mary met Jesus face to face on the lonely, painful path to his death. Mary would have been there. We know from Scripture that Mary's "fiat," her "yes" to the Holy One, forever marked her as a faith-filled woman of God. This woman had birthed a beloved child and she would surely have been there to take each bloody step her son took. She would not have shown up only at the final stage of his death to stand beneath the cross. Mary was too loving, too courageous, too risk-taking, too compassionate to have tended Jesus only in his final hours of hanging on the cross.

A key word in the traditional fourth sorrow is "meet." The root word of "meet" is *metan,* meaning "to come together, to encounter." When Mary met Jesus on the road to Golgotha, she "came together" with him. It was an intimate entwining of pain with pain. His suffering flowed into every part of her. Mother and son were together again, as closely knit as once in her womb. Mary felt his suffering in her own body and spirit. She went toward him, to meet this pain and to enter into it with him. This movement toward his pain came from the depths of her maternal love.

Not long ago I heard a mother describe her own modern-day story of literally meeting the pain of her twenty-one-year-old daughter. This mother's story bears a powerful resemblance to Mary's fourth sorrow. Carol's daughter, Sylvia, was living at home with her. One day Sylvia came home after taking care of an errand. She parked the car in the driveway and had just closed the car door when she was grabbed from behind by a man who demanded her money with a knife pressed to her neck. Sylvia reached in her pocket but had only a few dollars to give him.

Sylvia's attacker was angry at this and shoved his knife into her neck, cutting her carotid artery. While he ran away, she managed to struggle to the front door and ring the doorbell. When Carol opened the door you can imagine what she saw — a daughter dying before her eyes. Carol used every nursing skill she had to save her daughter's life, and months after the surgery and slow healing of Sylvia's body she continued to enter into her daughter's pain, walking with her on her road of suffering as Sylvia tried to also mend her inner world.

Another mother described how the discovery of a brain tumor in her twelve-year-old son led her to Mary. She explained how Mary helped her to meet the suffering of her son and of her own heart. The morning before surgery she was at prayer and she saw Mary's journey "all too clearly." She asked herself, "How did she walk to Calvary? Where did she find the strength? How will I walk with my twelve-year-old son through what is to come?" She was surprised at how drawn she was to Mary because for years she had found the rosary "monotonous and boring." She said she always felt that Mary was far removed from her on a throne in heaven, but in the space before her son's surgery, she realized that "Mary was the only one who could understand where I stood at that point in time. Mary, woman and mother, could give me the strength I needed to give my son as he faced life or death."

When we meet the pain of a loved one, we enter into it. It is there before us, demanding our attention. We walk the journey of pain and distress that another takes. We meet others in their moments of heartache and desolation in such a way that we, too, feel what they are experiencing. We are affected by how they hurt. We try as best we can to give them our love, our strength, our hope.

The fourth sorrow of Mary gives us both teaching and inspiration in learning how to meet the pain of others and our own pain, as well. It was in the life-moment of Mary's fourth sorrow that she came face to face with one of the most desperate situations that a mother could ever know. It was there that she looked upon unbearable suffering. It was on this journey to Golgotha that she let her son know by her presence that her love was with him, that she would be walking every step of the way as she entered into his passion and death with him. When we are meeting pain, whether it be that of one we love or our own pain, we are walking in the footsteps of Mary as she walked with her son on the long road to the hill of crucifixion.

Meeting Our Own Pain

Mary's fourth sorrow is about meeting someone who suffers. This "someone" may be a person whom we know and love. It may be a neighbor or an acquaintance who chooses to confide in us. It may also be a stranger whom we attend in our work of medical care, counseling, pastoring, or education. It may be a group of people who are a part of the world's suffering community. It may also be our very self whom we encounter on the road to Golgotha.

It is one thing to enter into the historical event and be there with Mary in her suffering. We can feel with Mary and honor her part in that potent, transforming event. Yet, we can also remain objective, maintaining a certain distance, allowing this event to be only a legendary or historical encounter. It is quite another experience if we see Mary reflecting our own life, Mary as one of us meeting the suffering of our self or the suffering of another. When we meet our own suffering or the suffering of another with the love with which Mary met Jesus, we are compassionating ourselves by entering into the heart of the pain.

The fourth sorrow of Mary can have tremendous value for us if we see it as a marker of one of the stations of our own life. Mary as Mother symbolizes the part of us that meets hurt and suffering on our own pain-filled journey. This maternal quality within us gives us the ability to extend a deep, loving gaze upon our own wounds. Our suffering offers us an opportunity to grow, to change, and to be spiritually transformed through it. This will not happen, however, unless we meet our pain in a compassionate way and willingly spend time with it.

It is essential, both on a spiritual as well as a psychological level, to enter into our own pain. Until we do so, we are never fully healed. We ought not deny it, bypass it, bury it, or ignore it. In order to grow, we must meet our own struggles and receive them with an attitude of openness and a desire to be healed. This deliberate meeting of our pain is where spiritual transformation finds its yeast. Jack Kornfield writes that many people first approach the spiritual journey "hoping to skip over their sorrows and wounds, the difficult areas of their lives.... [However], true maturation on the spiritual path requires that we discover the depth of our wounds." If we do not do this, we will find ourselves repeating patterns of our woundedness, such as unfulfilled desire, anger, and confusion.*

Very few persons want to come face to face with what is painful, messy, broken, and bruised in their lives. How much easier it is to avoid what needs healing, to turn away, and to go toward legitimate forms of busyness because it is simply too overwhelming to meet our suffering head on. Mary met the bloodied and disfigured Seed of her womb with great tenderness and love. Something in us refuses to do this. We tend to move away from, rather than toward, what hurts us. We choose to disconnect from it rather than to approach our suffering with compassion and care.

When my father died it took me at least six months before I was able to compassionate myself. He died just at the time that I was finishing work on *Praying Our Goodbyes.* I had done a lot of research on grief and, strange as it may sound, I thought that if I knew all about it I wouldn't hurt so much. If I just "knew enough," I'd be free from the prolonged sadness and emptiness that come with grieving. I didn't want to hurt. I hoped to avoid the painful components of grieving. Once I realized that I had not let myself into my own suffering, a door opened and I was able to embrace my sorrow, do my grieving, and eventually return to a more joy-filled life.

It is usually easier to enter into someone else's pain than it is to enter into our own. We can allow ourselves to get totally involved with someone else's suffering, so much so that all of our compassion goes in that direction while none of it remains for ourself. It may have to be that way for a while, but eventually we will need to tend to our own suffering, too, if we are going to be healed. Carol, Sylvia's mother, told me that she fully met the distress and terror that was a part of Sylvia's attack. However, she ignored

---

*Jack Kornfield, A *Path with Heart: A Guide through the Perils and Promises of Spiritual Life* (New York: Bantam Books, 1993), 41–42.

her own hurt. She kept telling everyone "I'm okay. I'm doing fine." One day a friend said to her, "You're doing fine? Then why are you not sleeping, not eating, smoking too much, and irritated with everyone?" It was time for Carol to tend to her own hurt.

Avoidance of suffering is obvious in those who find it nearly impossible to be with others in their times of great hurt: not visiting the sick, avoiding the bereaved, never speaking to another person about his or her illness, relationship struggle, work difficulty, depression, or any other painful situation. The avoidance is much more subtle when it is our own huge gap of pain that we need to encounter. We can easily make excuses for not taking time to pray in deeper ways because we fear awareness of how we truly think and feel. We can rationalize that we are so busy tending to someone else's distress that we have no time for our own. We can tell ourselves that it is silly or stupid to feel as we do. We can hide behind shame or blame, anger or hostility, insisting that what we suffer is someone else's problem and not our own. We can deny our addictions and weaknesses. We can let our fears loom so large that we succumb to doing nothing at all about what needs to be faced in our own time of suffering. By avoiding what is hurtful in our life, we cast aside a source of personal transformation.

We simply are not aware at times that we are treating our suffering as an enemy. I recall an eighty-year-old woman religious who wrote to me from her convent in a foreign country. Her letter was filled with pain. She related how much trouble she was having with her residence. She had lived and worked at one place for twenty-two years and, in her words, "did not realize what it was going to cost" when she moved to a community retirement center in a different region. She was miserable there and moved to a smaller convent and was miserable there, too. There was much discouragement, anger, and frustration in her letter. I could read between the lines how much she was unaware of the emotions of grieving that accompany such a great change and was, thus, unknowingly fighting the painful process of moving into the unknown terrain of her retirement. I longed for her to look upon herself with great love and to realize that she needed to comfort herself during the unsettling process of retirement instead of blaming herself for her decisions.

How Do We Meet Our Pain?

What is it like to meet our own pain? How do we do this? We must first believe in the value of encountering our pain. From this follows a deliberate intention of actually moving toward rather than away from it. If we are Mary meeting our suffering, it might mean that we enter into a recovery program for alcoholism, or seek therapy to heal a childhood memory, or speak with our spiritual director about a relationship struggle, or attend difficult meetings instead of conjuring up reasons not to be present, or dialogue with community leadership instead of simply judging and complaining about decisions or styles of leadership, or go for medical treatment even though we may feel vulnerable and helpless in the process. To be Mary meeting her suffering son on the way to Golgotha might involve our finally being honest with ourselves about such things as our jealousy, our self-pity, our exhaustion, our resentment, or our dishonesty.

As we become willing to meet our pain face to face, we need to embrace it with a compassionate heart, to meet it with love and tenderness, no matter how beaten, broken, or unwanted it may seem to us. We need to be as kind with our pain as we would be with someone else who is suffering. Pema Chodron, author of *Start Where You Are*, emphasizes that compassionate action has to start with ourselves. She writes: "It is unconditional compassion for ourselves that leads naturally to unconditional compassion for others. If we are willing to stand fully in our own shoes and never give up on ourselves, then we will be able to put ourselves in the shoes of others and never give up on them."*

It is a challenge to be with the unwanted, offensive stuff of our lives. It takes much courage to meet what seems, initially, only to bring us more distress and hurt. Mary, meeting her son, entered into tremendous turmoil and heartache. Yet, she also poured out intense love and encouragement. She never stopped loving her rejected and abused child. Her gaze of love took him in with acceptance and with profound acknowledgment of the hurt he was enduring. Surely her loving presence brought deep comfort to him as he struggled to complete the walk to the hill of crucifixion. We must tend to our own hurt in a similar manner, approaching ourselves lovingly, honestly, tenderly, with courage, and with confidence in our ability to complete the journey to deeper transformation.

There is another facet to this dolor that can also teach us how to meet our own pain. Scripture tells us that a great number of people followed Jesus on the road to Golgotha: "...and among them were women who were beating their breasts and wailing for him" (Luke 23:27). Mary was not alone as she met Jesus on the way. She was also not alone as she stood beneath his cross. Others were there who entered into her sorrow. They walked with her and they stood with her as she bore the great pain of her son's death. Their presence helped Mary to endure the raw edges of her pain. Their presence assured Mary that she could go through the agony of it.

A letter came one day and in it was a tender story of one sister helping

*Pema Chodron, *Start Where You Are: A Guide to Compassionate Living* (Boston: Shambhala, 1994), x.

another to enter into her suffering and be healed. Both women are in their sixties now, and one day when they were together for lunch Nell shared something she had never spoken about before. She told Anne that she felt a deep burden because she was the only one who couldn't remember any childhood memories when their siblings gathered for family celebrations. She "felt she had failed in her love of family by not caring enough to notice what had happened" in their lives. Anne had a big lump in her throat, but she went ahead and risked helping Nell to heal by recalling the pain in Nell's early childhood, how her polio from eight months old on took up all her energy and focus. She reminded Nell that she had not taken her first steps until she was five years old and that "her growing up years were very difficult."

As Nell listened to Anne she reentered her painful childhood. Nell saw things that she had not wanted to meet again. As Nell met her suffering, however, she also met her freedom, because Anne helped her to see the "why" of her loss of family memories. Nell realized in a much clearer way what a struggle life had been for her. Anne gave Nell a great gift of love by inviting her to enter those old memories of her pain. Several days later, after their conversation, Anne received a phone call from Nell, who said "I will never be able to thank you enough for what you told me about my early days."

We will find it extremely difficult to endure the tough process of encountering our suffering if we do not have at least one other person to stand with us, to weep with us, to encourage us, to never give up on us. How necessary it is to have others walk with us as we face the struggles that will lead to our growth. Knowing this, we can take courage in facing what needs our attention.

Trusting in the compassion of those around us, as well as in the compassion within ourselves, we can meet our pain and attend to it. We can risk being with the uncomfortable and unwanted emotions that reveal themselves when we look into the eyes of our own hurt if we remember how lovingly and nonjudgmentally Mary beheld her suffering son on his pain-filled road of desolation. With Mary as our mentor and our symbol of courage and compassion, we can meet our cross and be transformed through it.

I Speak to Mary

Mary, you have been there before me.
Your heart opened wide to embrace Jesus
when you met your son on his way to death.
You felt the depth of his suffering.
You entered his wounded path of pain.

I, too, need courage and spiritual stamina
to be with the pain of my own journey.
Teach me how to be with my suffering.
I want to meet myself as lovingly
as you met your wounded and pain-filled son.

Woman of Compassion, Mother of Sorrows,
I draw inspiration from your journey.
I, too, can move through the pain of my present situation.
Your faith and courage lead me to my own.

Meeting My Own Pain

Tender and loving God,
I know that you are with me.
Take my hand and stretch it
toward that which brings me hurt.
Lead me into my sufferings
and help me to be healed.
Together let us touch my woundedness.
Together let us meet my pain.

Teach me how to enter my suffering in a way
that brings me greater wisdom and growth.
Gift me with determination not to turn away.
Help me to meet myself with kindness and mercy.
Tender and loving God,
together let us walk the road to my healing.

Compassion for Self

Unwavering Love,
when I am going through troubled times,
help me to attend to my own spirit.
I need to believe that my heartaches
are also worthy of a compassionate gaze.
Teach me how to offer kindness
to the part of me that hurts.

With your grace I can overcome
any obstacles that keep me
from being attentive to my own needs.
Remembering your great love for me,
I turn toward myself with understanding
and reach out with tenderness
as I lovingly embrace my hurting self.

Encountering Depression

Giver of Life,
I am in the wasteland of depression.
I cry out to you, Source of Solace,
as I meet this empty void within me.
Sustain me as I try to exist
in this day-to-day dying
of my energy and vitality.

Wrap your arms around me.
Carry me through this bleak journey.
Help me to stay open to your love.
I rely on you. I lean on you.
I trust you to hold me close
as I stumble on this joyless path.

Meeting Physical Pain

Crucified One,
you endured tremendous physical pain.
My body, too, cries out for relief.
I look upon your experience and remember
that the Holy One will give me the power
to be with my suffering.

Teach me how to live with pain that cannot be alleviated.
May I find what is needed to tolerate it.
When possible, may I lean into this pain and learn its lessons.
Let me not be resentful of those whose bodies are free from pain.
When I arise each day without a release from my bodily hurt,
turn my heart toward you to draw strength from you.
When I try to sleep at night and the pain does not ease,
embrace me with the comfort of your presence.
Listen and draw near to me, Compassionate God.

Walking with Someone Who Suffers

Attentive and caring God,
you hear the cries of those in pain.
There are people everywhere who walk
a path filled with suffering and sorrow.
I have the privilege and challenge
of journeying with _____ .
It pains me to be unable to take away the hurt.
It saddens me to be unable to alleviate his (her) burdens.
Help me to not be afraid to be there with the pain.
Let me not run from what distresses and disturbs me
when this suffering invades my peace and happiness.

I want to be generous with my attention and my care.
May your Spirit guide me so that I will make good choices
about how much I can be and do for _____ .
Do not allow me to become so engulfed with the suffering
that I lose my balance and my ability to be with his (her) pain.
Bless all who walk with someone who suffers.

Guided Imagery (for one who walks on the road of suffering)

Begin by quieting your self.

Take a deep breath. Let the breath out slowly. Do this three or four
   times.

Relax. Be at ease.

Remember that you are held in the arms of God's protective love.

Go inside and find a place that has a long, desolate road.

Notice the dead trees, the huge thorns on bushes, the dry, stony soil.

It is the road of your own suffering. See yourself walking on the
   road. . . .

Feel the struggles that are yours. . . . Sense the power of your
   suffering. . . .

Look up now and see Mary coming on the road toward you.

She walks toward you with her arms open to receive you.

Go toward Mary and let her embrace you in your pain.

Let her compassion wrap around you. Let her love soothe your
   hurt. . . .

Walk hand in hand with Mary on the road of your suffering.

Tell Mary about your hurt, about what causes you the greatest
   suffering. . . .

Ask Mary what you need to do in order to be with your own pain. . . .

Now Mary reaches down and picks up a bright green oak leaf.

She holds it out and offers it to you.

Listen as she speaks to you:

"I give you this oak leaf
to remind you of the strength of the great tree.
You are like a tall, sturdy oak.
You have much courage within you.
You can meet suffering in yourself and others
and not be destroyed by its ravages.
You will have strength to do what you need to do.
Your sorrow is my sorrow. You are not alone."

Receive the oak leaf from Mary.

Stay with Mary for a while. Thank her for being with you.

Bid her farewell, and then slowly come back to this time and place.

For Personal Reflection and/or Group Discussion

1. Think of a life experience when you met suffering in the life of someone else.

   Can you see any similarities between this and Mary's meeting Jesus on the road to his crucifixion?

2. What is hardest for you in meeting the pain of others?

3. Think of a life experience when you met your own pain.

   How did you meet this pain?

   What was most difficult for you in meeting your own pain?

   Did meeting your own pain eventually help you in some way?

4. What does "being compassionate to self" mean to you?

   Do you agree or disagree with the idea that it is essential to extend compassion to yourself?

   What is the difference between self-pity and being kind to one's self?

   What would help you to be kinder to yourself?

5. Has your relationship with God influenced how you meet suffering in yourself and others? If so, how?

6. If Mary was sitting with you now, what would you want to say to her or ask her about this fourth sorrow in her life?

The Fifth Sorrow:
Mary Stands beneath the Cross of Jesus

STANDING BENEATH THE CROSS

. . . standing near the cross of Jesus were his mother, and his mother's sister, Mary the wife of Clopas, and Mary Magdalene. (John 19:25)

Mary Speaks

My heart was broken before we ever reached the place called Golgotha. Each pain-filled step that Jesus took pierced my heart. I felt sure that my son would collapse and die on the way, so slow were his steps, so labored his breathing. But each time he fell, he managed to stand up again, becoming more bloody and dirt-smeared every time. It was more than a mother could bear, but somehow I did not break completely. That deep, inner strength I have always relied on was there for me on that unforgettable day. It was a divine gift of courage I desperately needed.

I have no idea how long it took to reach the hill where they crucified criminals. I do remember begging the soldiers to let me be there with my son once we reached the place. They finally agreed, and as I stood there in my intense aloneness, supportive arms came around my shoulders. I turned and saw that

Mary Magdalene and Mary, wife of Clopas, had come to be with me. As they each embraced me, their ache and grief mingled with mine. Not long after, the disciple John came to join us, his tear-streaked face telling of his sorrow. The presence of these three brave souls comforted me in my desolation. I knew they felt my son's pain as well as my own.

The soldiers pushed Jesus down onto the large pieces of wood and nailed him to it. It was unbelievable that one human would do this to another. When they lifted the cross straight up, my son's tortured moan tore at my womb. My child! The horror of his agony overcame me. I let out a gut-wrenching scream, outraged at what was being done to him. Once that guttural cry escaped, I wailed no more during those long hours beneath his cross. My son needed my presence and courage. I knew I could give him those gifts in his dying. My grieving could wait. I stood inside his pain and I kept whispering to him, "My love, I am here. I am with you."

It was agonizing to hear the soldiers degrade Jesus with taunts and mockeries. Another wave of sadness washed through me when I saw some of those same soldiers rolling dice to see who would get the beautiful seamless robe I had woven for my son. I couldn't believe they would do this while he hung there dying. Just as I was thinking this, Jesus groaned in pain again, and I quickly said to myself, "It is only a robe, only a robe."

I shall always remember my son's touch of tenderness in those long hours of pain. Silent tears streamed down my cheeks when Jesus lifted his head and looked at me. I saw the kindhearted son I knew so well in that gaze. He turned toward his beloved friend John, and then back at me. His voice was hoarse and cracked as his dry mouth worked to get out a few words, asking John to take care of me and giving John to me as my son. My heart bled at the beauty of my son's kindness and at the finality that his words implied.

My vigil beneath the cross felt endless. I could see my son's life ebbing, but *his suffering continued. He grew increasingly weak, and his head hung lower. At one point, his face twisted into contortions, and his eyes rolled. Then, with unbelievable strength in his voice, Jesus cried out, "My God, my God, why have you forsaken me?" I wanted to plead with him, "Oh son, no, please, please do not despair. You are not being forsaken. The God you revealed is with you. In spite of what has happened here, you are not abandoned." But I remained silent. He was suffering tremendously, and I understood why he cried out as he did.*

Instead, I tried again to give him strength to make the final journey. He was so close to death. My voice was barely a whisper, for life had all but drained out of me, too. Yet, I urged my son, "Go, go to the Abba, the One you've come to know so well. Go home, my love, go home. Your work is done. You will be at peace." Soon after, Jesus raised his head slightly one last time, took a shallow, gasping breath, and uttered his last words: "Into your hands, I commend my spirit."

His final words told me he had come to peace with his suffering. It was over. My beloved son was dead. I would wonder no more what Simeon meant when he said to me: "and a sword will pierce your soul." The deed was done. My heart would be forever marked by it.

Standing beneath the Cross

There is so much suffering in our world. Everywhere people stand beneath heartbreaking crosses as they experience the excruciating pain of watching someone suffer. Like Mary beneath the cross of her beloved son, all that they can do is "be there" and wait with the one who is hurting, offering their love and support.

Many of us have stood beneath the cross. Sometimes it is the cross of disease and death. If you have ever accompanied someone dear who went through medical test after test, succumbing to the ravages of cancer, and watched the dwindling and destruction of his or her body, you have been at the foot of the cross with Mary. If you have ever had to place an aging parent with a debilitating disease in a facility for the infirm, you know what it is like to stand beneath the cross. If you have been a parent and had a child die in an unexpected, harsh, or violent way, you have known the heartache of Mary as she watched Jesus die. (Perhaps the most forgotten parents are those whose sons or daughters are the perpetrators of horrendous crimes. These parents, too, stand beneath the cross as they watch helplessly while their children are tried and convicted.)

The "crosses" we stand by may not always mean that the one who hangs there is physically dying. If you have listened and listened and listened to a friend who is journeying back through old wounds, you have been there beneath the cross. If you have lived with someone so depressed that he or she gave up the desire to live, you have stood on the same hill as Mary. If you have watched someone you love become devoured by drugs or alcohol and heard the denials and false promises, you have had a place beneath the cross. Any time you have been with another person who is suffering and have been unable to take the pain away you have been at the cross with Mary.

When we stand by the cross, we do not know what will happen to our loved one. Death may be immanent or death may be a large, looming possibility with hope for life still within reach. No matter what the outcome, our vigilance can be a powerful experience of deepening our love. A father of a twenty-two-year-old daughter told me how she had a severe asthma attack, and the doctors were not certain they could save her life. Both he and his wife agonized for days as they waited to see if she would recover. He told me that Mary's "be it done to me according to your will" was a strength for him during this time. He knew that his love for his daughter was deep and true and he longed for her to live, but he also had to accept what would be. His daughter did recover. As he reflected on the long vigil, he said, "I remember holding my daughter when she was well enough to give me a hug. What a joy that was when she said, 'I love you.' Never have those words meant so much to me."

Inner Strength and Resiliency

Mary *stood* beneath the cross of Jesus. In itself, standing all that time would have been extremely exhausting. Add to it the heartache and sorrow of seeing and hearing a loved one die — how much strength this standing had to have taken. The standing posture of Mary tells of her courage and fortitude. In *The Four-Fold Way*, anthropologist Angeles Arrien describes this posture as that of "the Warrior." "Standing" is a way to become more aware, to be present, to develop endurance. It belongs to one who has a brave heart, relies on inner power, and has a willingness to take a stand for what is good and true. This posture speaks of determination and inner strength to do what needs to be done.*

Mary's stance beneath the cross speaks of all of these aspects. Her long vigil there also speaks of faithfulness. Mary had the inner strength to endure the long wait. She stood as a warrior would stand, determined to do what she needed to do for her son. She was alert and totally present to the intense suffering that he experienced. Mary's presence at the foot of the cross is a vivid commentary on the resiliency of the human spirit. When love is the motivation, one can wait beneath a cross for a very, very long time.

---

*Angeles Arrien, *The Four-Fold Way: Walking the Paths of Warrior, Teacher, Healer, and Visionary* (San Francisco: HarperSanFrancisco, 1993), 15–24.

This ability to both physically and spiritually stand in faithfulness is a part of many people today as they vigil with a loved one who is seriously ill. It was certainly a part of Donna's experience when her husband had a heart attack which physicians failed to diagnose when he was first brought into the clinic. Dan had excruciating pain, and Donna described how she "stood vigil for over ten hours and never thought of sitting down" as she timed his pains "like a coach for a woman in labor." Donna said that the call had come when she was at work so she was wearing her work clothes, which included hard-soled patent leather shoes that were not made for long periods of standing. She emphasized that she "stood in those exact shoes for all those hours keeping vigil over my husband — my best friend and lover. I held his hand, talked him through the pain, made sure the ER staff monitored him frequently, gave him invisible strength, kept him company, and prayed that the physicians would finally diagnose the cause of his unbearable pain." Donna's husband survived his heart attack. As Donna reflected over her vigil by his side she concluded: "I feel someone was watching vigil over me at the same time I was watching vigil over Dan. And you know, I still have those shoes I wore in the ER that day, and they still hurt in airports!"

It is not easy to vigil with someone who suffers greatly, least of all when it involves being with someone who means much to us. It requires faithfulness, and it requires endurance. Whether it is our own cross or someone else's, some things simply have to be gotten through and endured. We need to be able to hold out, to bear up under tough times and not be destroyed by the process. Like Mary, we will need a courageous spirit and much inner strength to withstand the pain of being with the long vigil. We will find strength to "stand there" because of God's grace.

A wife whose husband was in the throes of a second bout of severe clinical depression felt his struggle immensely. While she grew tired of "being his Number 1 cheerleader" through the long months of his illness, she also longed to be able to take his deep hole of emptiness away from him. She wrote: "I felt tremendous sorrow at seeing the person I love suffer so terribly. I so very much needed to feel God's presence as we struggled through that tough time." Like Mary, she knew the value of spiritual strength to help her withstand the strain of being with her loved one's pain.

I think that one of the worst hurts is to be with a beloved who is suffering intensely and to be unable to take that suffering away. No matter how deep, strong, and enduring our love is, there are times when we have to accept how little we can do for the one who suffers. This is certainly true for all who are by the bedside of someone who has intense pain. It is also true in numerous other situations. Parents can comfort and console a child who is rejected, but they cannot force others to accept their child. Spouses can support and encourage a partner in a stressful job, but they cannot take away the emotional duress. Justice and peace workers can strive to change systems and standards of living, but they must also endure seeing what disease and starvation does to people before the systemic changes happen. Dedicated teachers can work with lethargic, disinterested students, but they are able to do little about the dysfunctional living conditions in which they live.

"Being There" for Others

From time to time, all of us are called to be with others who hurt, to support them in their struggles, to encourage, comfort, and console. Their painful situation asks us to patiently wait with them, to cheer them on in their valiant efforts, to extend mercy and forgiveness, to inform with kindness and understanding, and to be present in a nonjudgmental way.

Sometimes there is really nothing we can do except to "be there" for others who are in the throes of great hurt. When Marlene's good friend was falsely accused of sexually abusing a student she had taught some twenty years earlier, she tried to be there for her friend. She kept encouraging her friend not to lose hope even though she could do nothing to change the situation. Marlene wrote: "My phone bill to her is very large and my car has many miles on it because I strongly believe in physical presence as a major source of support. My friend tells me that my being with her gives her courage to face each new day."

We underestimate the value of "just being there." In our production-oriented Western culture it is difficult for many of us to really believe in the power of simply "being there" for someone else. There's a voice in us that keeps insisting that we have to *do* something. This voice questions the effectiveness of presence. I face this often in my own life. Is it enough to just listen? Is it sufficient to sit by the bedside? Shouldn't I bring something? Can't I say something that will make a difference? Something deep inside keeps trying to convince me that if I just know the "right" thing to say or do, then both the hurting one and I will feel better. Sometimes words do help, but many times it is just "being there" that is most comforting and helpful.

Another difficulty about "just being there" with a hurting person is that we will feel that person's suffering. It is a tremendous challenge to be a compassionate person because when we are truly "with" the hurt of another, when we enter into that person's pain, it is not a distant, removed sort of thing. Who would choose to deliberately enter into suffering? Some may be there initially, but very few will hang around for "the long haul."

I recall a man in his thirties, highly successful in his business profession, who refused to visit his father who was in the hospital almost two months with life-threatening complications from cancer surgery. His excuse was: "I can't stand to be around pain." If he could have gotten beyond the barrier of his own aversion and fear of pain, his presence at his father's bedside would have been a great comfort and aid to his father's healing.

Part of what makes "being there" difficult is that we can get caught up in our ego. Our ego is afraid of looking foolish or sounding stupid. Thus, we grow fearful and worry if what we say and do, or don't say or do, will be the wrong thing, that we'll look bad, or we won't be able to help the other person. ("I don't know what to say at funeral homes. I'm afraid to mention her divorce. I didn't want to bring up her late husband's name.") Other people can also make it more difficult for us to be present beneath the cross. A woman in a religious community vigils with prisoners on Death Row. She said that more than once someone has said to her, "Can't you find something better to do with your time? He deserves what he's getting."

We may not realize the value of "being there" for a long, long time. For almost two years I vigiled as a spiritual guide with a woman who was in a dark hole of depression. I heard her angry and futile attacks on herself, her rage and disappointment with life. I saw her sink deeper and deeper into self-repulsion and obsessive guilt over past failures. I felt her loss of psychic energy. It pained me greatly to see a vibrant, intelligent, creative woman caught in the tangle of a harsh opponent like clinical depression. In the midst of standing by her cross, I held the container of hope and self-affirmation for her. I believed for her when she couldn't believe for herself, and I kept the vision of her eventual recovery ever before my spiritual eyes. I trusted in the new life that I felt could eventually be hers if she was willing to stay in the process.

It was not easy. I grew tired of her being so self-disparaging. I wanted her joyful and happy again. I didn't like her refusal to hope. It tugged against my joy and pounded on my own beliefs. I didn't know what else to do to help her out. I wanted to run but I stayed. I just stayed. I kept being there for her whenever she came. It was the best thing I could do and, as it turned out, it was the right thing to do. When she recovered, she thanked me for carrying the vessel of hope for her when she had holes in her own.

Others Who Stand with Us

Mary embodies the faithfulness of divine compassion. She waited as her son slowly died. Her heart never left him as he suffered the dreadful brokenness of his crucifixion. Although Mary could do nothing to stop the execution of Jesus, surely her presence beneath the cross was a comfort and an encouragement to him as he hung there dying. The courageous presence of his mother was a wordless message of her unfailing love for him.

When actor Christopher Reeve had his life-changing accident on his horse, it paralyzed him from the neck down. He said there were many moments early on when he wanted to die, but the words of his wife, Dana, restored his courage and have ever since given him the desire to live. She said to Christopher, "I want you to know that I'll be with you for the long haul, no matter what."

It is important to note that Mary did not stand alone. She had the comfort and strength of the three who waited with her. We also need others to be with us in our Golgotha moments. Whether we hang on our own cross or stand beneath another's, we can be overwhelmed by intense emotions and feel a chasm of acute loneliness. Having others who compassionately stand with us gives us the inner stamina to hold up under the emotional weight of what we are experiencing.

I have had several times in my life when I have felt hung on the cross. During each of these agonizing times I have been blessed with kind and understanding friends, colleagues, and therapists. It made all the difference to me. Their presence took away some of the loneliness and softened the unwanted emotions that came with the hurt. Their compassionate stance gave me courage to be with my cross and not hide out in my self-pity and grief. Their patient vigiling gave me the strength to not give up on myself.

Mary: The Vigilant One

The woman who stood beneath the cross had been weathered by the storms of life. It was not the first time she had suffered intensely. By the time Mary stood beneath the cross of her dying son, she had known many seasons of distress. She was a willow tree who had endured numerous wild winds, always bending resiliently in the fierce adversities of her struggles. The limbs of Mary's spirit had grown stronger and her roots deeper as she experienced her many sorrows.

Some who are tried by the storms of life become bitter, hardened, angry victims. They pull in on themselves, grow tight, and shrivel up in a small corner of resentment. Others, like Mary, grow expansive hearts. Their suffering helps them to be more open and available to others' hurts and struggles. They know what it is like to experience pain, and this lived knowledge carries them lovingly into other people's lives.

Mary was consistently changed by her sorrows. She was a walking story of love, transformed by the pain that she not only endured but pondered and integrated into her faith-filled life. From the time of her "fiat" when she said "yes" to the mysterious Voice in her life, she knew that she had within her a power much greater than herself. Time after time she had to reach within and draw on this inner strength. In sorrow after sorrow she had to believe that there would be a dawn of hope after all the turmoil and pain.

Florida Scott-Maxwell, in her memoir *The Measure of My Days,* writes at age seventy-five: "Love opens double gates on suffering. The pain of losing good is the measure of its goodness."* The more fully we invest in another, the greater our sense of deprivation when we lose that person. The more we love and the stronger our commitment, the deeper our loss will be. Mary knew this in her profound love of her beloved child. She never knew it as fully as when she stood beneath his cross.

---

*Florida Scott-Maxwell, *The Measure of My Days* (New York: A. Knopf, 1968), 42.

I Speak to Mary

Mary, you have been there before me,
weary and worn out from the long vigil,
saddened by the pain of your loved one,
heartbroken over what you could not change.

Your valiant stance beneath the cross
tells me of your unceasing love.
Long years of unfailing faith upheld you.
Kind friends by your side sustained you.
I, too, am standing with a loved one
who hangs upon the cross of suffering.
I, too, am powerless to help.
Teach me how to stand beneath this cross.

Woman of Compassion, Mother of Sorrows,
I draw inspiration from your journey.
I, too, can move through the pain of my present situation.
Your faith and courage lead me to my own.

Strength to Endure

Enduring Love,
now is the time
for me to stand strong,
to remain vigilant,
to stay with the pain,
to continue to be present.

Giver of Strength,
firm up the wobbly legs
of my faltering faith,
reinforce my trust in you.
Intensify my ability
to not give up.
With your grace
I can remain faithful.
No matter how powerless
or hopeless I might feel,
I can be a compassionate presence
as I stand beneath the cross.

When Someone Vigils with Us

Jesus, Son of Mary,
you knew how much pain and grief
your situation caused your mother.
Even as her presence comforted you,
you looked upon her great sorrow.

When I feel guilty or selfish about
those who stand beneath my cross,
when I want to shut them out,
or try to keep them away
so they won't hurt so much,
remind me to let them in.
They need to be there for me,
and also for themselves.
Let me be big-hearted enough
to welcome those who want to help.

The Comfort of Others

Companion of the Suffering,
the touch of your embrace
comes to me in the gift
of those who stand with me.
How grateful I am
for the compassionate ones
who wrap me in their care,
and console me with their kindness.

Source of All Love,
what encouragement is mine
in those you have given to me.
Thank you for their thoughtfulness,
their patience, their empathy.
When they stand with me,
I know in a more certain way
that you have not abandoned me.

The Heart of Compassion

Compassionate God,
your generous presence
is always attuned to hurting ones.
Your listening ear is bent
toward the cries of the wounded.
Your heart of love
fills with tears for the suffering.

Turn my inward eye to see
that I am not alone.
I am a part of all of life.
Each one's joy and sorrow
is my joy and sorrow,
and mine is theirs.
May I draw strength
from this inner communion.
May it daily recommit me
to be a compassionate presence
for all who struggle with life's pain.

Standing beneath Another's Cross

Crucified One,
it is never easy,
this standing under the cross
of one who hurts.
When I doubt my ability
to say or do what is best,
guide and direct me.
When the pain of the situation
seems too much to bear,
strengthen and support me.
When I feel helpless and alone,
remind me of how near you are.
When I grow weary and impatient,
fill me with your love.

May all who hang upon a cross
of suffering,
or stand beneath one today,
find comfort and consolation
in your abiding presence.
Ease their suffering.
Free them from discouragement.
Gentle their anger.
Cease their restlessness.
Coax them away from despair.

Guided Imagery (for one who stands beneath the cross)

Begin by quieting yourself.

Take a deep breath. Let the breath out slowly. Do this three or four
times.

Relax. Be at ease.

Remember that you are held in the arms of God's protective love.

Go inside.

Look for that emotional place within you that needs courage and
resiliency.

Let yourself be in this place.

See Mary come to be with you.

Notice her inner strength, how it permeates her whole being.

Feel the aura of her immense love. . . .

Tell Mary about your journeying with someone who is suffering.

Be honest and open about your thoughts and feelings. . . .

Notice how lovingly Mary listens to your story.

You can see that she knows what you are experiencing. . . .

Let Mary tell you how she managed to endure standing beneath the
cross of Jesus.

Listen to what sustained her during that excruciating time. . . .

Now Mary extends her hand toward you. She is holding a gift for
you.

It is a small, smooth stone. Let Mary place the stone in your open
hand.

While you hold the stone, Mary speaks to you:

"Please accept this gift from me.
It is a courage stone, a symbol of divine strength and endurance.
This stone will remind you that you have these gifts within you.
This may be difficult for you to believe when you stand beneath the
    cross.
You must trust that the enduring courage you need will be there for you.
I understand your difficult situation.
Your sorrow is my sorrow. You are not alone."

Let yourself be permeated with the strength of Mary's love. . . .
Let your fatigue, discouragement, and powerlessness slip away
    from you.
Rest. Be at ease.

Stay with Mary for a while and then thank Mary for being with you.
Bid her farewell and slowly come back to this time and place.

For Personal Reflection and/or Group Discussion

1. When have you stood beneath the cross of another? What was this person's suffering like?

   Describe what your experience of standing beneath the cross was like for you.

   Was anyone else there beneath the cross with you?

   What was most difficult for you when you stood beneath the cross?

2. Where do you find your inner courage and strength?

3. Have you ever had a time when *you* were on the cross and someone vigiled with you? If so, describe this experience.

4. What is most helpful for you when you are supporting another who is suffering?

5. Has your relationship with God influenced how you have experienced standing beneath the cross? If so, how?

6. If Mary was sitting with you now, what would you want to ask or say to Mary about this fifth sorrow in her life?

The Sixth Sorrow:
Mary Receives the Dead Body of Jesus

EMBRACING OUR LOSS

Joseph of Arimathea, who was a disciple of Jesus, though a secret one because of his fear of the Jews, asked Pilate to let him take away the body of Jesus. Pilate gave him permission; so he came and removed his body. (John 19:38)

Mary Speaks

All the people who stood at a distance had gone away. It was nearly evening by the time Joseph of Arimathea came with permission to take down the dead body of my son. I had waited and waited by the cross, not wanting to leave for fear they would take Jesus without my being able to embrace him one last time. As Joseph and another man carefully took his body off the cross, I asked them to let me hold him. I knew they had to hurry to the tomb because of the Sabbath's nearness, and I promised them I would not be long.

They protested: "He will be too heavy for you. He is covered with blood. It will be too much for you." But I insisted. I had to hold my son. I opened my arms and made my lap wide. "Please" I said again, "do not deny me this last touch of a mother's love." They brought Jesus to me then.

How awkward and weighty his body was as they placed him on my lap. All the time I stood beneath his cross, I had longed to touch him, but when I finally was able to do so, his body was lifeless and cold. Still I cradled him, held him, rocked him as best I could. I wept tears of relief that his suffering was finally ended. I wept tears of desolation, knowing that he was truly gone from me.

My hands encircled his head as I kissed his swollen eyes. My tears fell into the gashes on his cheeks. As I rocked back and forth with the dead weight of my son in my arms, a stream of memories pushed into my tears. I watched Jesus nursing at my breasts. I looked at him eating his first solid food. (I remember how much he liked bread.) I saw his first steps as he tried to walk. As the memories washed like a river through my mind, I knew again his deep brown eyes, flashing with sparks of delight as we walked through fields of flowers. Beautiful scenes of joy spun through my mind: our laughter over the tiny animals Jesus brought home in his pockets, the wobbly way he tried to hold the saw when he first helped Joseph in the shop. I recalled his uncanny questions at such an early age and his ability to find treasures in the most unlikely places.

All our times of sorrow and heartache also reached out to me. I thought of our great sadness when Joseph grew increasingly frail. (How gently he departed this life. He was such a good man.) I felt again the intense struggle of Jesus as he made his decision to leave home and go into public ministry. I lived anew those days when he surprised me with his visits, returning to me exhausted but at peace with what he felt he needed to do.

I whispered to my beloved son: "I have always been touched by the beauty of your spirit. Your goodness illuminated your face and radiated in your actions. No wonder so many people were drawn to you. Now I look at your maimed, destroyed body and waves of anguish clutch at my heart. I thought I had hurt in the other times of tribulation, but nothing, nothing could have prepared me for this moment. I can hardly bear to look at the condition of your body. Is there a place that is not wounded, bruised, cut open?"

The wounds of scourging and crucifixion hid his scars from childhood, but I knew they were there, all the scrapes and cuts he had gotten when he went exploring with his friends. I could "see" his inner scars, too, the rejections that hurt him as his public ministry developed, especially when those in our own village had shunned him. As I touched his hands, I recalled how they had reached out and healed the leprous outcasts, had blessed and broken bread, had lifted little children high into the air as he played with them. I stretched my hand to touch his feet and remembered how many places those feet had journeyed, how tired those feet were when he traveled from town to town. I placed my hand over his heart — the generous, merciful heart, slashed and deadened by those who did not understand or accept his message of love — and endless tears engulfed my sadness.

Painful, probing thoughts pressed in on me: Maybe if he had not been so vocal about changing cherished laws, maybe if he had not healed on the Sabbath, maybe. . . ." As I looked upon my son, I knew I did not understand some of the things he had done, but I had taught him to stand up for what he believed and he had done that. I had supported him when he left Nazareth, but when I held his dead body in my arms, how I wished he had never left home.

Then I felt a light touch on my shoulder. They were telling me it was time to go. They could wait no longer to take the body of my son to be entombed. I kissed Jesus once more, and then I let them take him from me.

Living Pietàs

Every life has its share of pain, struggle, and hard times. Mary's life was no different. The greatest hurt of Mary's life is artistically expressed in

Michelangelo's marble masterpiece, the *Pietà*, from the Latin word meaning loyalty and devotion. In this sensual, visceral work of art we see the poignant image of a mother holding the torn and ravaged body of her executed son. Both Mary's strength and immense love are portrayed through the face and posture that Michelangelo gives to her. In the *Pietà*, Mary has large, broad shoulders and a wide, generous lap on which the dead body of her son rests. The *Pietà* is a powerful reminder of how much strength love can have and how much pain it can evoke.

Mary gathered the dead body of Jesus into her loving arms, embracing him as one embraces a beloved who has been through tremendous agony. She not only drew his dead body to herself; she drew a lifetime of love, and all that he had suffered, to her heart. His pain was inside of her. There was an immense oneness between the mother who sat there and the crucified son whose body lay on her lap.

Mary received Jesus as one who compassionately receives the pain of the world or one's own great desolation. She held him as one who holds the horror of human tragedy and dreadful grief. She embraced him as one who embraces the deepest love they have ever known. Mary receiving the dead body of her son becomes a metaphor for any one of us, man or woman, when we open the arms of our love to receive suffering and death into our lives. By that generous gesture, we become living *Pietàs*.

I can never be with the *Pietà* for very long before I begin to resonate with the sufferings of others. I see Mary as a symbol for my own life, believing that I, too, am meant to receive others in their deep distress. The son whom Mary holds is a symbol of the suffering people in my life who need someone to be with them when they are vulnerable, sorely troubled, and overwhelmed with the intensity of life's painful unfolding.

The *Pietà* is a strong image of compassion. The figure of this sorrowful mother reflects all those who weep and grieve as they hold their great loss and pain close to their heart in a long, embracing farewell. When I gaze upon the *Pietà*, I see, not just Mary, but every person who has ever embraced and held the pain of another in the arms of their care. In Mary I see each of us, gathering to our hearts the weary and worn ones of the world. Never have we needed this inspiration more. Our world is filled with pain and distress. Everywhere there are hurting ones longing to be received with this kind of loving embrace.

We can understand the *Pietà* as a posture of our heart when we are caught in the grips of goodbye or when we are tending to others who are suffering grievously. The experience of the *Pietà* is everywhere in our world. Mary receiving the dead body of her son is every parent, of any age, who has suffered the loss of a child. Mary holding the crucified Jesus is every sorrowing person who embraces a loved one and bids a final farewell. Mary is everyone filled with anguish and sorrow who has held what has died in their life and wondered why it happened.

Receiving the Wounded Christ into Our Lives

The key word of this sixth sorrow of Mary is "receive," meaning "to take back." When Mary received the dead body of Jesus in her arms, she was taking back, receiving Jesus in his totality, with all the accompanying pain that came with holding his battered body. In that moment, Mary had come full circle with Jesus, receiving in death the bruised and beaten body of the son she had birthed as a fresh, healthy child some thirty-three years earlier. Everything she had known and cherished about her son, all the love they had shared, the trials and tribulations they had experienced, each hope and dream she had for him, all this Mary held on her sorrowing lap.

The wounded Christ in Mary's lap is also in the lap of our lives. The Jesus of the *Pietà* is each suffering person who enters our life. We may be receiving the dead body of someone we love or we may be receiving a nonphysical death (a great loss) that causes us, or someone else, immense grief. Being a living *Pietà* means that there are moments in life when we need to hold what has died, cherish what has been, and accept the reality of the pain that comes with this loss.

When we receive hurting ones, we gather them to our heart as Mary did and embrace them as a wounded Christ. We cradle them with care and reverence in the lap of our compassion. A lap is that part of us that we naturally have when we sit down; it allows us the ability to hold things there. A lap is a place of comfort where little ones are cradled, where children feel sheltered and protected. It is while lying on the lap of the mother that the child is nurtured and often where children are rocked to sleep.

Mary's lap was spacious. We, too, need space — spiritual, emotional, mental, and physical, — in order to receive another's pain, to give our attention to it and embrace it. Sometimes suffering is shoved into our lap. We do not expect or want the experience of receiving it. We would not choose to have it plopped into our lap, but there it is, whether we desire it or not. We may feel forced into being a living *Pietà* by a life situation that cannot be avoided. At other times, we deliberately open the arms of our love to embrace the one who bears suffering. At these times, we feel called to reach out toward that person's suffering, to receive it as Mary received her son. We still find it difficult, but we choose to do it. Anytime we reach out with love toward another person's suffering, we are Mary receiving Jesus into her arms.

One evening I was at a festive gathering to celebrate a special anniversary of friends. We gathered around an elegant table and dined on delicious food. I wanted to sink into the relaxed mood, sip my wine, and cherish animated conversation. But seated next to me was a woman filled with intense sorrow. Although she was a stranger to me, I quickly learned of her pain. Her only daughter had been killed in an accident a year earlier and I could feel the tremendous grief that consumed her.

Yet, as much as I perceived her pain, I did not want to be sitting next to her. I wanted to have an easy, joy-filled evening. I didn't want to form a lap of compassion for her suffering. I didn't want to be a listener to her pain that night. I realized what was happening to me as she talked. It took me about five minutes to open up the space within me, to bring my compassion forward, and truly enter into her sorrow. As I listened to her anguish of becoming instantly childless, I realized how selfish my initial response had been.

When we hold suffering ones in the lap of our compassion, we put our own agenda aside and receive them as they are. We let go of what we want to have happen and what we think should happen. We put aside our judgments of them and allow them to be with us as they are. We do not cast aside our thoughts and feelings, but we do not allow these thoughts and feelings to dominate or control how we are with this hurting one.

Our lap or inner space can get full, tight, too guarded. It can develop walls around it. We can become "too busy" to call lonely parents, to be concerned about ill friends, or to really listen to the hurt of a child. We can become too self-oriented to notice the distress of another or to put aside our joy for the sake of someone else. Fear of the cost, distaste for vulnerability, lack of belief in our ability to handle the pain, nonawareness of the hurt of another, and many other reasons enter into our inability to receive someone who suffers.

We also have to hold what has been injured or has died in our own life and give it our full, compassionate attention. We may need to receive the death of a dream of being "someone" or of having a certain "something" or someone as part of our life. We may need to let go of a hope to birth children when infertility is diagnosed, or acknowledge that our age no longer permits us to drive a car, or realize that our expectations for certain things in a job will not happen, or accept the reality that our religious community is dying. The "dying one" we hold may be the ending of an ongoing fantasy that has occupied us for much of our life, perhaps that of having the perfect relationship, the model family, or a wealthy lifestyle.

We hold death in the lap of our life both symbolically and literally. For some, their *Pietà* is an actual receiving of the physical body of another. There is the mother who found her teenage son hanging from a rope in his bedroom. She raced to the kitchen, found a knife, and cut him down. How Mary-like she was as she knelt there with her son in her arms, sobbing in horrified disbelief at her son's senseless death.

Another mother wrote to tell me of her eight-year-old daughter's death when she was riding her bike on a country road in Kansas: " . . . a pickup truck struck her, killing her instantly. A little white cross now stands where I picked up her shoes." Tears filled my eyes as I pictured this mother picking up those little shoes. This gesture is not unlike Mary's receiving Jesus into her arms. Pain is pain in whatever form it is received.

There are countless scenes that closely resemble the *Pietà*. Hospital chaplains see them often. One of these chaplains told me that the most emotional experience she ever had at work was the day she was in the ER waiting room and saw a young mother in a rocking chair that an RN had brought in for her. The mother was "cradling a gorgeous four-month-old baby girl" who had died of SIDS. The chaplain said what made it so heartrending was not only the death of the precious little one but that it had happened on the first day that her young mother had returned to her regular job. She said, "I stood there and cried as I saw how 'alive' the child seemed in her mother's arms. She was such a beautiful baby."

At other times it may not be a person who's died that we receive into our arms but someone who will always be ill or incapacitated, someone whom we daily clothe, feed, and tend as in the case of adult children who care for aging, infirm parents. If we can hold these aging ones as Mary held her beloved son, what a difference it will make in the compassionate way that we are with them.

The Difficulty of Holding Suffering

It had to have been excruciating for Mary to cradle the maimed and battered body of Jesus on her lap. Yet, she must also have yearned to hold him, to treasure the feel of his limbs, the closeness of his touch, the shape of his face, the contours of his body. To do so meant that she also had to hold his death, to endure seeing closely how the beating and battering had destroyed his flesh. The body Mary held in her lap was that of a crucified criminal with all its cruel markings.

The *Pietà* is not a romanticized, soft sort of thing. It hurts to enter into the *Pietà* of our lives. It is not easy to receive suffering into our arms. It can be a heavy burden just as the body of Jesus resting in Mary's lap was heavy and unwieldy. Suffering can crush us, press us down, weigh heavily on our minds and hearts. The suffering of others that we carry can be so large that we wonder if we can handle it. No one in their "right mind" would want more pain. But no one in their "right heart" would refuse it if it meant encouraging, strengthening, and consoling another human being who is in pain.

Some suffering is almost more than we can bear to receive. Physical deformities from fire, birth defects, cancer of the face, car accidents, and other afflictions that change physical appearance often intensify the pain of receiving the one who suffers. (I can still hear the mother who told me through her tears that she did not recognize her son after a car crash.) When Mary held the body of Jesus she must have been horrified to see the sores, the gaps, the ugliness of his body. It has been said of the crucified Jesus that he was like someone "from whom others hide their faces" (Isa. 53:3). Each of his wounds cried out as witness to what he had endured. Each gouge in his flesh left a wide crevice in his mother's heart.

Compassion requires that we allow the lap of our life to hold the suffering of others. We can do this only if we act from a center of love deep within ourselves. The *Pietà* is an intensely vivid reminder of how much strength this love has and how much power this love gives to do what needs to be done. No truly compassionate person can always keep a safe, objective distance, not even therapists, chaplains, and physicians. We cannot offer compassion and then decide to remain fully detached and separate. The pain of another will brush across our heart if we are truly "with" another. We will suffer with that person if we have genuinely become a compassionate being.

We are all called to receive the suffering of another in one way or other, no matter what our profession or life situation. The more we receive those who suffer, the more natural it becomes for us. The people I know who are most compassionate are often those who have had suffering in their own lives. Each experience of pain has opened them up a little more. The opposite can also happen. Each hurt can close us off. So much depends on how we approach our suffering and how we receive it into our lives.

Mary Holds Us in Our Suffering

When I was giving a retreat, a woman shared a beautiful story about Mary. This woman had painful back surgery, and after the surgery, she did not sleep for twelve days because she was in terrible pain. She said it was the first time she ever understood why someone would want to take their own life. At the end of the twelfth day she said to Mary, "Look, you are supposed to be my mother. You'll have to hold me and take care of me because I just can't endure this any longer." Then she adjusted the pillows under her feet and slept for ten hours without waking. She said that she was conscious of her pain while she slept but that it was tolerable pain and did not keep her from sleeping. It was the image of Mary's maternal love embracing her that gave her the ability to relax enough in order to rest in her sleep.

Mary opened her arms and widened her lap to receive her crucified son. It was a natural response for her because her entire being had always been open to him. The generosity of Mary's spirit inspires my own willingness to be with those who suffer. Her ability to receive suffering rekindles my own desire to be there for others, in an open and generous way. Her broad shoulders and her wide lap tell me that it is possible to enter into deep suffering and survive.

When Mary held Jesus that last time, she did not know where his body ended and hers began, so deeply was she united with him. When we are compassionately joined with the suffering of another as Mary was with Jesus, their great distress will resound in our soul. When our hearts are receptive and loving as Mary's was, we will embrace this suffering and know in a deep place within us what it is like to be a living *Pietà*.

I Speak to Mary

Mary, you have been there before me.
You opened your arms, your lap,
to receive the body of your son.
His scourged and crucified flesh told you
of the sufferings he had endured.
You held him as beloved, wounded child,
with all the pain a mother's heart could have.

I, too, have known loss in my life.
Teach me how to embrace this suffering.
Remind me of your generous lap
and the broad strength of your shoulders.
As I receive what is wounded
may I hold it as lovingly
as you held your child, Jesus.

Woman of Compassion, Mother of Sorrows,
I draw inspiration from your journey.
I, too, can move through the pain of my present situation.
Your faith and courage lead me to my own.

God's Embrace

Guardian of the Wounded,
wrap me in your embrace.
Hold me close to your heart
and assure me of your love.
Protect my sore spirit.
Ease the pain that it holds.

You are always ready
to embrace me,
no matter how hurt or desolate
my heart may be.
I will trust you with my pain.
I will rest in your solace.
I will take refuge in your love.

Heavy Burdens

Jesus, Rest for the Weary,
the heaviness of my burden
overwhelms me.
The immensity of this situation
presses down upon me.
The weight of the pain I carry
crushes my hopeful vision of life.
I long for an easing of my distress.

Let me hear again
your promising words of comfort.

Speak them to my heart:
"Come to me, all of you who are weary,
and carrying heavy burdens,
and I will give you rest" (Matt. 11:28).
I lean my burdened life
on the bosom of your love
and wait to be consoled.

A Generous Response

Generous Love,
create in me a welcoming space
where I will readily embrace
those who need my compassion.

Free me from selfish withholding
of my time and presence.
Clear out all resistance to giving
of my kindness and understanding.
May the generous availability
of your love for me,
influence and inspire
my loving embrace of others
who hurt and struggle.

Experiencing Loss

All-Embracing Love,
your circle of strength
is around me.

I ask for grace to yield
to the reality of this loss.
I pray to surrender
to what cannot be changed.
I beg for deliverance
from the emotional drain
and the unending sadness
that this loss has brought me.

Let peace return.
Let hope begin.
Let comfort be mine.

Companioning One Who Embraces Loss

God of strength and hope,
be with the suffering ones,
especially those who are
receiving a deep loss today.
Gently open their hearts
and stretch their capacity
to be with their great hurt.

I walk today with _____ ,
who is experiencing a significant loss.
May my presence with her (him)
be one of empathy and kindness.
Help me to be a living *Pietà*
of kindness and concern.
Draw me into your heart
so that your deep and strong love
will resound in my own embrace
as I receive _____ into my care.

Guided Imagery (for one who has received a significant loss)

Begin by quieting your self.

Take a deep breath. Let the breath out slowly. Do this three or four
   times.

Relax. Be at ease.

Remember that you are held in the arms of God's protective love.

Go inside and find the place within you that needs comfort and
   consolation.

Let yourself be in this place.

Imagine yourself to be in a lovely meadow.

Mary comes there to be with you.

Notice how kindly she looks at you. . . .

The two of you sit down in the meadow.

Let yourself be held by Mary.

Lean your head on her shoulder or put your head on her lap.

Feel her love, the easy quiet of her presence. . . .

Speak to Mary about your significant loss.

Notice how carefully and lovingly she listens to you. . . .

Let yourself receive Mary's comfort. . . .

Now Mary takes a soft shawl and places it around your shoulders.

She speaks to you:

"Receive this shawl.
When you are holding suffering in your life
remember that you have great strength within you.
May this shawl that warms and protects your shoulders
remind you of the shelter of the Holy One.
Your sorrow is my sorrow. You are not alone."

The two of you rise, the shawl still wrapped around your shoulders.
Walk together, hand in hand, to the edge of the meadow.
Stay there quietly for a while,
Thank Mary for being with you.
Bid her farewell and slowly come back to this time and place.

For Personal Reflection and/or Group Discussion

1. What meaning or significance do you find in the *Pietà?*

   Have you ever felt like a living *Pietà?*

   What do you find most challenging about receiving the suffering of another?

   What do you find most rewarding about receiving the suffering of another?

2. Describe a time when you had the suffering of someone pushed into your lap of life. How did this happen and what did you do about it?

3. As you reflect upon the spaciousness of your lap of love and your current life situation, how much room do you have for the suffering of others?

4. Has your relationship with God influenced how you have been a "living *Pietà*" for others? If so, how?

5. If Mary was sitting with you now, what would you want to say to her or ask her about this sixth sorrow in her life?

The Seventh Sorrow:
Jesus Is Laid in the Tomb

LAYING OUR SORROWS TO REST

Now there was a garden in the place where he was crucified, and in the garden there was a new tomb in which no one had ever been laid. And so, because it was the Jewish day of Preparation, and the tomb was nearby, they laid Jesus there.

(John 19:41–42)

Mary Speaks

As they carried the body of Jesus to the garden where he was to be placed in a tomb, I walked in a daze, totally bereft. Still, I was grateful because someone's kindness had again comforted me. After Jesus had breathed his last, I wondered what we would do about the burial. We were too far from home to return there and I knew of no place near the city to bury him. Then the man from Arimathea came to me and assured me that we could use his tomb for Jesus. I was deeply touched by his generosity. I wondered if this loving gesture was a message from my son who was always speaking about trusting the Holy One to care for us.

When we reached the empty tomb, I stumbled up to the entrance and looked inside. My heart sank at the finality of separation as the tomb's hollowness echoed inside of me. I turned back and saw that they had placed Jesus' body on a stone slab and were ready to wrap it for burial. Again I was grateful for kindness. A secret disciple of Jesus had bought a hundred pounds of myrrh and aloes. Together we blessed my son's body with the fragrant oil. As it spilled over his flesh, the abundance of it reminded me of the generosity of his goodness. Although I had wept so much before, many more tears came. They were tears of sorrow and tears of deep love. They were tears of gratitude for the gift I had been given in birthing and raising a child so filled with God-ness.

I was too exhausted to help them with the wrapping of the burial cloths. I tried but my weakened hands would not hold the cloth. As I beheld the tender way in which they wrapped my son's bruised flesh, it momentarily eased some of my grief. When they began to wrap his face, I took one last look and knew I had to let him go. It was not a new thing for me — the letting go. How many times I had chosen to let him go as he grew up, away from me, and toward his public ministry. I had never clung to him then, and I knew that he would not want me to cling to him now. It was finished. Jesus would want me to have hope in spite of my great heartache in losing him. I wanted to feel this hope but all I felt was sadness.

Just before they lifted Jesus to place him in the tomb, I bent down to kiss his wrapped body farewell. I did not doubt that he was at peace with the Abba he so lovingly described and prayed to, but this belief did not quench my sorrow. My son was dead. We were placing his body in the tomb. I could stay with him no longer. As I kissed him one last time, I felt his spirit embrace me. A surge of courage and love enveloped me as fully as the burial cloths that were wrapped around him. I stood up and had a profound sense that my son would always be with me. I knew then that it would be more than his memory that sustained me in the future. A part of him would remain in my life. I would always have a deep abiding awareness of his presence. We could entomb his body, but we could never bury his love and goodness. These rich treasures were mine forever and they would be a part of everyone who ever loved him.

Before I turned to leave, I placed my hand on the stone that blocked the entrance to his tomb. So much had happened in one day. I was drained and desolate. I saw sadness and loneliness in the days ahead of me. Yet, I knew that my heart would be at peace as time unfolded, that there would eventually be moments of joy again. I had listened well to my son, and his lessons were not lost to me. But joy was far from me as I walked away that day.

I thought of Joseph, dear Joseph. I yearned for him to be beside me as I left the tomb. His presence would have eased my emptiness. Joseph had been an endearing stronghold for me when life was strained. How I missed him at that moment. Jesus and I had both grieved greatly when Joseph died. We had consoling conversations about our loss. Jesus had tremendous hope for life after death and often said how much he looked forward to being united with the Holy One.

This truth did not lessen the void in my heart but it strengthened my desire to walk away from the tomb with confidence in my heart. I had said my "yes" to the Holy One when I was a young woman. I placed that "yes" in my footsteps of grief and resolved to trust divine love to once more help me find my way. Little did I know at that moment just how fully present my son would become to me or how clearly I would see the way. But I will save that story for another day.

Our "Tombs"

When Mary went to the garden where her son's body was to be laid, it was not the first time she had stood before a tomb. Her husband had died and she knew the loneliness and the struggles of widowhood. Some of her relatives and friends were deceased. She knew what it was like to say that final goodbye to someone she loved. But this time it was different. She was losing a child, the treasure of her womb. Mary's presence at the burial of her son would have been heartbreaking even if he had died of "natural causes," but what made it extremely agonizing was the untimeliness and harshness of his death.

So much of her life had been devoted to her son. Every mother knows how much attention, energy, and commitment is given to a child. The union or bond of a mother's love is a thread that runs through all of a child's life, no matter how old he or she is. The death of Jesus was un-doubtedly Mary's greatest goodbye. She had struggled with the decision to bear her child. She had questioned, wondered, pondered, and finally said "yes" to the Holy One. Once she had given her consent in faith, Mary never looked back. She gave herself fully to what was asked of her in birthing and raising her special son.

Mary's faith in the Holy One did not keep her from suffering. It did not shield her from the sorrow and loneliness that are a part of death, but it did keep her from being swallowed by the bitterness and hard-heartedness that can come when one has many tribulations. Mary, the mother, could never have been at the burial of her son and not known grief. She tasted it fully.

If you have ever stood by a casket, filled with emptiness and heartache, you have been at the tomb with Mary. If you have ever been overwhelmed by the finality of death and the loneliness it evokes, you have felt Mary's sadness. If you have ever wondered how you could cope with losing the one you loved the most, you have known Mary's grief. If you have ever felt exhausted and desolate by the experience of saying goodbye to someone you treasured, you know what it is like to be there at the tomb. If you have ever felt devastated and destroyed by a brutal life experience, you have made the journey with Mary because you have witnessed a death to some part of your precious self.

The "tomb" is any situation that insists we let go of what has given our life meaning and value. Many people have written or spoken to me about the tombs in their lives. Their stories are not always about physical deaths. A woman working in a bookstore described caring for her mother with Alzheimer's: "My mother is not here. I have let go of her. The woman I care for is mean, angry, hostile. My mother was gentle and full of laughter. I tell myself that I am caring for the mother of a friend, and then it doesn't hurt quite so much."

I read a news article about a man whose father had been a successful professor at a university until he eventually became mentally ill. He became a homeless person "in greasy, lice-ridden clothes," and the son tried and tried to get his father into treatment for his illness. When the son finally succeeded in doing so, the treatment had little effect on his father's behavior, and he eventually went back to living on the streets. The father this man knew was "gone." He had become entombed in paranoid schizophrenia.

Our tombs are not always about people. Many tears were shed when an old walnut tree fell in a wild storm, leaving sorrow in the hearts of those who had known its beauty and felt its comforting shade. When a woman preparing for retirement moved away from her beloved hills in order to be closer to her children as she aged, she fell into a dark hole of depression. She had not realized how much what she had left had shaped her life and given her happiness until she stood by the tomb of her farewells. She thought about selling her new home and traveling back to her old place but she knew, deep within, that her leave-taking was essential for what her future held.

There is a tremendous finality associated with the tomb: The lid on the casket is closed. The last of the divorce papers are signed. The homestead farm is sold. The letter of job termination comes. The breast is removed. The apartment is destroyed by a tornado. The endings go on and on. Over and over, the stone is placed in front of the entrance to the tomb. There is no returning to what once was. Not in the exact way that it was before. There is no way to undo what has been done. We cannot restore what has left us forever.

The tomb challenges our beliefs and taunts our hope. It puts our life in quick perspective. Death of a loved one can throw us off balance for a while, make us think we will drown in our grief. The experience of losing a loved one can feel like our greatest emotional enemy. In our grief, it is easy to forget about the Resurrection and the new life that follows closure at the tomb. Our faith in something beyond the finality of the tomb can strengthen us during our time of loss. It can gather us under the sheltering wings of the Holy One. It can assure us that our loved ones who have died are at peace. Our faith can give us reasons to have hope, but it will not keep us from the painful process of grieving. What faith does for us is to keep assuring us that we can go on, that we will one day know better times, that we will eventually have some space in our days without perpetual sadness and emptiness.

Leaving the Tomb

Faith helps us to let go. If we listen closely to the message of Jesus, we will hear him urging us to value what is good in our life but not to hold on to it so tightly that we forget what is beyond this life. Jesus taught his followers to invest in love. It is the one treasure that we take with us into eternity. It is the all-encompassing quality of the Holy One. Mary was a woman of love, par excellence. Her entire life was centered on this deep divine quality. This prevailing inner gift gave her the power to let go and to trust in life beyond this one.

When a loved one or something we greatly value dies, the letting go that is asked of us is an essential part of our healing. We cannot keep clinging to the past, holding on to what we once had. Even though life will not be as it once was, we can still go on into the future. We may not feel like we can, but it is possible to do so. We have a new life awaiting us. It will not be exactly like the one we have known but it can be a good life, with peace and happiness. This will not happen immediately. It could not have happened instantly with Mary. She left the place of burial as a desolate, mourning mother. We must give ourselves time and patience when we are grieving. Acceptance of our loss does not occur overnight. Alleviation of our sorrow is a gradual process.

No matter what age our loved ones might be, it can still be painful to let go of them when they leave us, whether this is through death or some other life event that takes them from us. My women friends have told me how hard it is for them to have their children leave home for a life of their own. They know "in their heads" that they cannot, and ought not, keep their children to themselves, but their hearts clutch at them, wanting them to stay bonded to home in a way that is no longer possible for a young adult.

On the other end of the spectrum of life, there are those who can't let go of their aging parents. Fear of their parents' death pushes some adult children into overly protective, controlling behavior. Some adult children take over their parents' lives long before they need to, dictating what their mothers and fathers should and should not do, treating them as if they had lost all ability to make good choices on their own.

Letting go can be all as painful as the experience of death itself. A mother told me how she came to terms with having to let her daughters go into their tomb in order to have a new life. After she discovered that her daughters had been the objects of incest, she was "like a fierce mother bear trying to protect them and help them heal." She was constantly aware of trying to do all she could to shield them from harm and comfort them from the emotional pain that had been inflicted upon them.

This caring, loving mother said that after years of doing this, she realized that the final healing for them would not come until she stepped out of the way. She confided: "I gave them as much as I could and I had to trust that they had their own strength. I could not do their healing for them. I had to release them to make their own journey. It was like watching them die while they were being reborn. I had to stop trying to fix it all and allow them to do their last piece of healing on their own. I had to let them enter their pain. When I let go of their journey, I could see peace coming for them."

Sometimes we want to hang on to our hurt after a person dies. Something in us says we ought to hurt forever if we really loved this person. So we perpetuate our sorrow by never letting it go. We keep activating it by continually telling our story or creating situations so the pain persists. I saw this happen in a mother whose young daughter had been killed in a car accident. It was a horrible scene in which the eleven-year-old was thrown from the vehicle and impaled on a fence post. Her mother carried photos of this accident, and everywhere she went she took out the photos and showed them to others. When she showed them to me it had been many years since the accident. It was time to put the photos away.

Other people perpetuate the story of their "tomb time" in order to draw attention to themselves and to receive affirmation. They become the "whining victim" who's had it tough, continuing to be hurt, nursing the wound, and spending all of life talking about it. They never allow their loss to be yeast for their spiritual transformation. When stories of loss and tribulation are told ceaselessly for years, it is a sign that there is some letting go yet to take place.

There are also situations where loss happens in such a way that it is next to impossible to bring full closure to the tomb time. This is especially true for those whose loved ones have disappeared and are presumed dead but their bodies are never found. Those who have experienced political rebellions, wars, or crime-related losses know how excruciating this can be, always uncertain about the fate of their relatives who have "disappeared." There can be no final closure for them. Rituals help, but the person who grieves often has a sense of incompleteness. Such is the case of a woman whose sister has been missing for some twenty years. She wrote to me: "Pieces of her clothing were found but nothing more. Even though we had a ritual of goodbye, I still wonder whether or not she is alive somewhere. This thought returns often to haunt me."

Sorrow Shapes Our Future

When Mary walked away from the tomb, her life was marked forever. For as long as she lived, her son's death would influence her journey. The Scriptures do not tell us how this happened, only that Mary was at prayer with the disciples in the Upper Room at the time of Pentecost (Acts 1:14). Perhaps she never went back to her home in Nazareth once she walked away from the tomb. Mary may well have joined those who were active in spreading the message of her son, serving as a beacon of wisdom and hope for the early Christian community. People would have been drawn to her as they were to her son because her presence reflected his generous love. Her compassion was enhanced and deepened by the sorrows she had lived.

Suffering has the potential of giving us tremendous wisdom and new direction for our lives. I can still hear the beautiful music that came from the front of a large conference room in Los Angeles. I had just entered the room to speak to a group of fifteen hundred catechists, and I was immediately drawn to the beautiful sounds coming from the piano. The music created a welcoming atmosphere for those of us who gathered. Before my talk, I thanked the older man who had been playing the piano. When I did so, he told me his story.

He had been a successful CEO when he developed Parkinson's disease. He struggled with staying at work until it was no longer an option for him. At first he was desolate and despairing, but gradually he turned to something that had long been a great love of his: creating and playing piano compositions. He told me that he was happier than he had ever been even though he still struggled from time to time with his disease and its limitations. From his "tomb time" had come a new source of joy. He had allowed sorrow to shape his life in a positive way.

I heard a similar story from a woman named Jane. She enumerated her "tomb times" that had taken place during one year: her mother's death, the sale of the family farm, and the loss of her teaching job. Jane said, "Broken in spirit, I finally abandoned my career in education and began training as a licensed practical nurse. This was the beginning of resurrection for me. I spent twenty wonderful years in this profession." Likewise, a happy middle-aged man told me that it was only after his parents' death, which was a deep loss for him, that he found a new inner freedom and began his work as a passionate, colorful artist. He said that the seed of his art was always there but it took the death of two dear people to awaken and trust the seed within him.

The many sorrows of Mary shaped her future. The same is true for us. The sorrow that comes with death marks us in some way. Our life will go on but we will never be quite the same. Our "tomb times" change us. They can bring us wisdom, develop compassion in us, and move us in new directions that call forth unknown talents and revitalized generosity, or they can stunt and maim us for life because we refuse to accept the finality of the tomb and move on from it.

Moving On into the Future

Moving on does not mean that we never look back. Mary certainly looked back after her tomb time. She would have needed the memories of her life with Jesus to sustain her during her time of grieving. She would have needed the strength of their conversations to help her believe in his lasting presence on those days when she missed him terribly. We need to move on into our future, and yet we do not need to abandon the beauty and goodness of what was once a part of our life. Good memories are precious reservoirs of hope.

My Christian faith assures me that Jesus rose from the dead and that he appeared to various of his followers. There have been many scholarly discussions about whether or not this was a bodily appearance of Jesus or a spiritual one. Perhaps it makes no difference. What seems evident to me is that Mary was so closely united with her son that she would always have a profound sense of his presence in her life. She could never forget the spirit of his love nor the power of his goodness. All that she had learned and experienced from her life with him would gift her walk into future days and years. We, too, must take the best of what has been and gather it to our hearts. No matter how painful the circumstances of our "tomb time," we do not need to leave our good memories in the past.

Mary had to have patience and hope, as we all do, when we have placed what we have loved in the tomb. I remember a father of a son who committed suicide commenting to me: "There's this intricate net that you call your life and suddenly there's a huge hole in it and you feel that no matter what you do, the net will never be mended." The hole in Mary's net must have been very large, too. It is not easy to leave the tomb with so much hurt in one's heart. But there comes a time when we have to walk away and look forward more than we look back. We, too, need to choose when and how to move on with our lives, confident in our inner resiliency and in the abiding strength of God's presence with us. Mary has been at the tomb of farewell before us. She knows the finality of it and she knows how to walk on from there. She can show us the way.

I Speak to Mary

Mary, you have been there before me.
You have stood at the tomb and said your goodbye.
I, too, am facing an ending in my life.
Like you, I need to turn away and move on,
believing that the Holy One will console me.

You know how grief engulfs the heart
and tries to strangle the joy it contains.
You have felt the drain of a great loss
and the empty hole that it creates inside.
Teach me how to have confidence
when I question what the future holds.
I, too, want to be strengthened by my faith
as I let go and move on with my life.

Woman of Compassion, Mother of Sorrows,
I draw inspiration from your journey.
I, too, can move through the pain of my present situation.
Your faith and courage lead me to my own.

At the Tomb

Companion of the sorrowful,
be my strength
as I say my goodbyes.
Be my courage
as I face what needs
to be let go.
Be my patience
as I trudge along
through empty days.
Be my consolation
as I carry sadness
in my heart.
Be my hope
as I turn from the tomb
and walk into the future.
Be near, O God, be near.

Prayer of the Desolate

Comforter of the desolate,
the pain of my loss goes deep.
There is a huge hole in my life,
a rip in the garment of my heart.
I cry out in anguish,
knowing you will not forsake me.

God of the sorrowing,
draw close to my desolate soul.
Mend the hole in my heart.
Give me strength to go on.
Bend your compassionate ear
to the sadness in my heart
and hear my cry for help.

One Who Is Lonely

Eternal Presence,
you are with me on my journey.
You know the loneliness
that wraps around my heart
and leaves a void of sadness.
Comfort me on my dreary days
when emptiness is all I know.
Do not let me succumb
to isolated self-pity.
Let me experience your presence.
Fill my downcast spirit with your joy.
Keep me close to your abiding love
with every step I take.

Embracing Hope

Loving Gardener of Life,
turn my time of sorrow
toward a season of hope.
I long to return to joy.
I yearn to be free from sadness.
May the eyes of my faith
look beyond my loss
and see the promise of spring
that follows every winter.

Never-Ending Source of Hope,
may the power of the Resurrection
assure me of future happiness.
I hold out my downcast spirit to you
and offer you my trusting heart.
I await the healing I need,
confident that your grace
will restore my inner peace.

Walking with One Who Mourns

Holy Shelter,
I walk with one who grieves.
Help me to be patient
with his (her) journey of loss.
Let me not rush or push
the process of healing.
Grant me the gift of insight
to know when to speak
and when to be silent.
May my words of advice be few
and my loving presence ample.
May my heart reflect
the fullness of your compassion.

Heart of Consolation,
ease the sorrow.
Relieve the aching spirit.
Bring your soothing solace
and comfort him (her).

Guided Imagery (for one who is grieving)

Begin by quieting yourself.

Take a deep breath. Let the breath out slowly. Do this three or four
times.

Relax. Be at ease.

Remember that you are held in the arms of God's protective love.

Go inside.

Look for that place within you that needs comfort and consolation.

Imagine that you are in a cemetery.

Find a tombstone that reminds you of the loss that you feel.

Sit down by the tombstone and allow your grief to be present....

Look up and see Mary coming to be with you.

She sits down beside you and holds your hand.

You can tell that she understands your hurt.

Speak to Mary about your grief, tell her what hurts the most....

Mary sits quietly with you.... Then she speaks to you about your
loss....

Ask Mary any questions you have and listen to her response....

Now Mary lets go of your hand.

She invites you to hold it open to receive a gift she has for you.

As you open your hand she gently places a small, brown seed in your
palm.

Then Mary speaks this message to you:

"I know your sadness. I am sorry for how you hurt.
Please receive this tiny seed.
Let it be a reminder to your sorrowing heart
that there will be new life for you.
Just as this little dry seed holds new life inside it, so do you.
In time, peace and joy will return to your heart.
Keep hope close to you. Don't give up. Joy will return.
Your sorrow is my sorrow. You are not alone."

Hold the seed and stay with the message for as long as you like.
Let the message take root in your heart.
Thank Mary for being with you.
Bid her farewell and slowly come back to this time and place.

For Personal Reflection and/or Group Discussion

1. What have some of your "tomb times" been (significant endings and farewells)?

   Make a list of them.

   Do they have anything in common?

2. Choose one of your "tomb times" and respond to the following questions:

   a. What have you had to let go because of your tomb time?

   b. Has this experience shaped or influenced your future?
      If yes, how?

   c. How has your relationship with God affected how you have gone through this tomb time?

3. When you have been hurting in the past, where have you found hope?

4. If Mary was sitting with you now, what would you want to say to her or ask her about this seventh sorrow in her life?

EPILOGUE

When I first thought about writing this book four or five years ago, I had a growing belief that those who suffered could find solace and comfort in the seven sorrows of Mary. I felt that if they could recognize their pain in the sorrows of Mary they would find both strength and hope because Mary's experience is so real and faith-filled. Yet I continued to question whether this was a valid conviction or not. I kept asking myself: Just because I've experienced Mary in this way, will others also find her sorrows meaningful for their lives?

Then, as I entered into the process of writing the book, things occurred which convinced me that there truly is a strong thread between Mary's sorrows and ours. As I met with the elders of my community a great hope stirred in me, whispering that I was "on the right track." Each time retreat and conference participants sent me a story of a sorrow in their life that was similar to Mary's, I also felt more confirmed in my belief. There were, however, two significant events that deepened my conviction more than anything else. One of these happened when I finished the first draft of the book and the other took place a week after I had sent in the completed manuscript.

Soon after I had written the first full draft of this manuscript I went to Frontenac, Minnesota, to join with seventy others in a week-long experience of the Dances of Universal Peace. Before the dances began each day there was always an opportunity in the early morning for various forms of communal prayer. In mid-week the facilitator announced: "Tomorrow morning the prayer will be centered on Mary's joy and sorrow."

I was amazed at this because those who gathered for the Dances were quite a mix of Sufis, Buddhists, Jews, Catholics (both Roman and Orthodox), and Protestants of many denominations. I wondered how the prayer would evolve and who might choose to attend. At 6:30 a.m. I yawned my way up the mile-long walk to the building where the prayer was to take place. As I walked into the room, I was surprised by how many others had also come. We waited in easy silence in the crowded room until the leader invited us to reflect upon the life of Mary. We began by thinking of Mary's joy at being the mother of Jesus. Then we imagined ourselves as a young pregnant Mary, her body full and round. We walked contemplatively around the room with Mary's fullness, rejoicing as she had done, in the powerful mystery of life that was within each one of us.

We sat down again and were invited to think of Mary's sorrow at the death of her son. Then our leader asked us to ponder our own sorrows and burdens. She gave us a long space of silence to enter into these hurts and concerns. After this period of quiet, we were encouraged to "cradle" these sorrows, to hold them in our arms, and to walk in silent procession from the room on third floor down to the statue of Mary that stood on the spacious green lawn in front of the red brick building.

Once we arrived in front of the statue, I was astounded. Here was a tall, partially blackened, wood figure that reminded me immediately of the Buddhist image of Kanon that I had met in Kamakura, Japan, two years earlier. The look on Mary's face was so much like Kanon's, the same gaze of peace and the same deep compassion. I looked down and saw that this wooden depiction of Mary was firmly rooted in the ground. I discovered later that the wood itself used for this particular statue of Mary was a tree that had caught on fire when it was struck by lightning. Woodcarvers who had gathered for an annual convention one year saw the remains of the tree and carved the beautiful black Mary from the tall trunk which was standing as a silent, wounded sentinel on the front lawn. "Ah," I thought, "even the wood itself has suffered, but out of it has come a symbol of compassion and hope."

As we stood before Mary, our leader invited each of us to come and lay our troubles and sorrows at her feet, to "let them go," to "give them to Mary." What happened next also astounded me. A young woman stood by the side of Mary and began to wail. Several men bent down before Mary and opened their arms to empty their burdens and each began to weep. They remained there for some time. I saw and heard more and more tears as each person bent to give their burdens to Mary. It was a powerful moment for me, to see how deeply the connection with Mary's sorrow had touched their hearts. Surely each one who left their sorrows and heartaches at the feet of Mary that day had a sense of how Mary had suffered and how deep was her compassionate understanding and love.

The second event took place the week after I sent in the completed manuscript of *Your Sorrow Is My Sorrow*. I had flown to Northern Ireland to facilitate a five-day retreat at Benburb. We were just into the first full day of the retreat when the terrible news came that a bombing had occurred in the town of Omagh, less than forty miles away. The bomb had killed thirty people, including two unborn twins, and had injured over two hundred others. I will never forget being with the retreatants that first day as I listened to their pain. Many were from the North and some had relatives and friends in Omagh. One retreatant had five relatives killed in the bombing.

Many of those on retreat were devastated by the news. They had thought that the new peace accord would finally hold. After years of fear, mistrust, and constant siege, the people of the North were beginning to believe they would finally have a land of peace. On the day of the bombing, hope dropped out of their hearts. Discouragement etched its way across faces and sliced its way into distraught hearts. Sadness, gloom, and frustration came through their voices. It was a terribly difficult moment. I felt their pain and I gathered their loss to my heart as best I could, knowing that I could not undo their desolation or stop the river of hopelessness that was once more raging within them.

It was not just the retreatants and not just the North but all of Ireland that was caught emotionally in the shock of the Omagh bombing. Everywhere people felt sick of heart about it. They were outraged to think that a small radical group could brutally undermine their hope. It was in the midst of this emotional atmosphere that I opened the *Irish Times* newspaper six days after the bombing. There I read about a young woman, injured in the bombing, who had just given birth to her first child, a healthy six-pound girl. Another fact was also given: in a country where division and hatred between Catholics and Protestants had a strong history, this little girl had a Catholic mother and a Protestant father.

I later discovered that every major newspaper in the country included this news item. Why? Because in the midst of sorrow, human beings stretch to touch a thimbleful of hope. In the turmoil and struggle of brutal loss, the human heart pleads for some sense amid senselessness. In the emptiness of pain, the human spirit longs for a glimmer of love. It was not only the birthing of a tiny child who had been in her mother's womb when a bomb exploded, it was also the powerful message that here was a family where division and hatred had not taken root. Peace *was* possible.

It is this kind of hope that I believe was firmly fixed in Mary's heart. Her sorrows also seem brutal and senseless. Why would a king with so much power try to destroy a helpless child? Why would the authorities murder her son when he had healed and helped so many of the people in the territory they governed? Why would a kind and loving person who had always reached toward peace be treated as a monumental threat to peace? Mary's hope was also shattered, but she did not give up. She searched for that tiny glimmer of hope amid the destruction, and she went on with her life, continuing to be a loving and compassionate woman.

It is out of these life experiences that I have become convinced that all who have suffered, or have walked with someone who has suffered, can say to Mary:

> In the tears of your life, I see a reflection of my own tears.
> In the struggles of your life, I see my own tribulations.
> In the desolate places of your life, I see my own attempts to regain hope.
> In my yearning to find someone who knows what it is like to bear these burdens of mine, I look into your life and I see your shock, your fear, your emptiness, your confusion, your desolation.
> Yes, I know now that your sorrow *is* my sorrow.
> And I see, too, that you withstood all that brought you pain and heartache.
> I see that you found a wellspring of strength within you.
> I know that it is possible for me to also find this deep source of encouragement.
> I, too, can find a place of peace and hope within myself.
> The Holy One who sustained and sheltered you will also sustain and shelter me.
> I am not alone.

A NOTE FROM THE ARTIST

Working on drawings for this profound and thoughtful book has become an unexpected blessing. The invitation came so unexpectedly, reconnecting me at once to my family and earlier years. How could I not say "yes"? Both Mom and Dad were very devoted to Mary, and my sister, three brothers, and I were raised on the Rosary and Sorrowful Mother Novena. Just months ago we honored my mother's desire to be buried in her Third Order Servite habit.

As I read the manuscript, something reaches into places within me still vulnerable from my close relationship to Mom in her years of diminishment and recent death. Both the reading and the drawing are a providential grace, enabling me to feel and pray deeply the heaviest sorrows of my present life. These are three, which are clearly interwoven for me: the weight of Mom's physical and spiritual suffering; the painful awareness of the unparalleled suffering of planet Earth — both in our violent destruction of her life systems (environment) and the sufferings of her people; and lastly, living with my own shattered dreams and physical and spiritual losses. It is as if while I read and work with the drawings for *Your Sorrow Is My Sorrow,* the sorrows I secretly carry are being prayed and held and healed in the great Mary Heart of the World. I am blessed and grateful.

MARY SOUTHARD, CSJ

La Grange, Ill.
September 1998

About the Author

Joyce Rupp is well known for her work as a writer, spiritual "midwife," and retreat and conference speaker. A member of the Servite (Servants of Mary) community, she has led retreats throughout North America, as well as in Europe, Asia, and Africa. Joyce is the author of eight books, among them *May I Have This Dance* and *The Cup of Life* (from Ave Maria Press), *The Star in My Heart* (from Innisfree Press), and *Dear Heart, Come Home* (from Crossroad Publishing Company).

About the Text Artist

Mary Southard is well known for her work as a visual artist, educator, and "student of the Earth." A member of the Sisters of St. Joseph of La Grange, she works in a variety of media — paint, plaster, paper, crayon, clay — and is best known as a creator of the Earth Calendar. A catalog featuring some of her work is available from her community (1-800-354-3504).

About the Cover Artist

Ted (Ettore) De Grazia (1909–82) became internationally known as "the people's artist" in 1960 when UNICEF selected his image "Los Niños" as its Christmas card, which holds the record for most sold of its kind. The De Grazia Gallery is located in Tucson, Arizona.

ALSO BY

JOYCE RUPP

—■—

DEAR HEART, COME HOME
The Path of Midlife Spirituality

"This book is an act of pure poetic kindness on Joyce Rupp's part. In sharing personally, she helps us become more gentle with ourselves and others, and more intimate with God. It is unique, filled with warmth yet at the same time practical and challenging. Classic Rupp!" — Robert J. Wicks, author of *Seeds of Sensitivity*

0-8245-1556-0; $13.95

Also available on audiocassette:
CHANTS AND VISUALIZATIONS TO ACCOMPANY
DEAR HEART, COME HOME

Two audiocassettes: 0-8245-3013-6; $18.00

—■—

Please support your local bookstore, or call 1-800-395-0690.
For a free catalog, please write us at
THE CROSSROAD PUBLISHING COMPANY
370 LEXINGTON AVENUE, NEW YORK, NY 10017

We hope you enjoyed
Your Sorrow Is My Sorrow.
Thank you for reading it.

crossroad